the Power of Protein

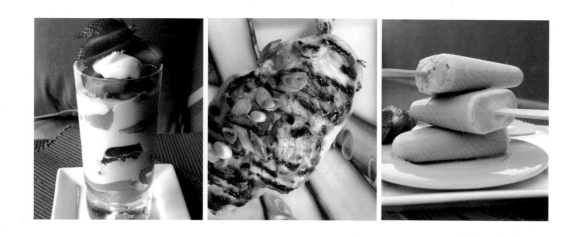

First published in Australia in 2007 by
New Holland Publishers (Australia) Pty Ltd
Sydney • Auckland • London

1/66 Gibbes St, Chatswood NSW 2067 Australia
218 Lake Road Northcote Auckland New Zealand
United Kingdom The Chandlery , Unit 114 50 Westminster Bridge Road London SE1 7QY

Reprinted in 2012, 2013, 2014

A record of this book is held at the National Library of Australia.
www.newhollandpublishers.com

ISBN: 9781741105704

Publisher: Martin Ford
Project Editor: Lliane Clarke
Designer: Tania Gomes
Production Manager: Olga Dementiev
Printer: Everbest Printing Co Ltd (China)
Photographs: Alison Blake

20 19 18 17 16 15 14 13 12 11

the Power of Protein

Losing Weight with a High Protein, Low Carbohydrate Diet

Chris Smith

Acknowledgments

First of all I would like to thank you—the readers. Your feedback has been fantastic and so invaluable to me in presenting this *Power of Protein*. I am sure you will love the illustrated recipes and enjoy cooking them. Each recipe has its individual carbohydrate count so that you can still ensure you stay within your guidelines.

Once again a special thank you to my good friend Leanne for her friendship, her patience and her clever ideas with solving problems and enabling us to bring you a variety of food and maintain our low carbohydrate lifestyle.

To Hi-Lo Homewares thank you for allowing us to use your beautiful cookware, plates and accessories.

Finally to my dear family and friends thank you so much for your love, friendship and support—it means everything to me.

Discovering the Power of Protein

When I first heard about the low carbohydrate, high protein diet, I thought, like most people, there had to be something wrong—it was the opposite to what I'd been taught, but I also knew that counting kilojoules and following a low fat diet didn't work for everyone. So began my research—only to discover this way of eating is hardly new. It takes us back in time—to our ancestors—those hunters and gatherers—those people with good strong bones and little evidence of major diseases. Look at our own Aborigines—the ones who haven't been introduced to the modern high carbohydrate foods and you will still find strong healthy bodies.

Go back to the traditional Eskimos and take note of their diet, very high in meat, fish fat and water and not only were they healthy and slim, heart disease and diabetes were unheard of.

I am neither a dietician or a nutritionist—all I've got to offer you is my experience—eighteen years of helping people lose weight. What this has shown me is that for the vast majority of people this is the easiest and most enjoyable way to do it—without hunger and without depriving you of good tasty food and if there is anything I have learnt after eighteen years in the weight-loss industry it's this: what suits one person is not necessarily right for another—DIFFERENT STROKES FOR DIFFERENT FOLKS—FIND WHAT WORKS FOR YOU AND STICK WITH IT.

This book came about because so many of my friends and clients kept saying all they could find on the subject was either too technical, or the ingredients for the recipes were not readily available here—so here it is in everyday layman's terms.

Plus a range of recipes—some from my friends—some from clients and some of our old favourites revamped to keep the carbohydrates low.

CONTENTS

THE DIET

THE RECIPES

A Message to You

The information contained in this book reflects the author's experience only and is in no way intended to substitute for any advice given to you by your medical practitioner.

This information is not intended for people with specific medical conditions or pregnant or nursing mothers.

If you are an insulin dependent diabetic or taking prescribed medication, you must consult with your physician before undertaking any change in your diet as any change could affect your medication and result in serious health problems.

Before commencing this or any other weight loss plan you should consult with your medical practitioner.

In the event you use this information without your doctor's approval, the author assumes no responsibility as you are prescribing for yourself.

WELCOME TO THE POWER OF PROTEIN

In the following pages you will be shown how to lose weight by following a Low Carbohydrate (CH)/High Protein diet in a very simple format. We don't want to confuse you with lots of technical jargon so you will find this book simple and easy to use.

The recipes are suitable for many people who have either lost weight or just enjoy the benefits of following a Low Carbohydrate/High Protein lifestyle.

For those of you who still need to lose weight and are on a restricted number of carbohydrates you will find all the recipes have the appropriate number of carbohydrates counted for your benefit. This is an easy way for you to stay within the count allocated to you.

Should anyone be concerned with fat content you may substitute with low fat alternatives but be aware that many 'low fat' products contain added sugar. Even the smallest amount of extra sugar will take your body out of 'fat burning' mode.

HOW THE DIET WORKS

Quite simply, we consume food usually with too many carbohydrates (more than your body can burn). If your body does not burn these extra carbohydrates it will store them. In most cases your body only has the capacity to store these carbohydrates for 48 hours—some people for a little longer. If you haven't used them in that time the body processes them through the liver and turns it into fat. Now you are storing it permanently—as fat.

Picture a storeroom in your body, filled with carbohydrates.

When we lower our carbohydrate intake our body still needs energy, so it will use what is in the storeroom first, providing you do not give it any high carbohydrates, and then turn to the stored fat for energy.

You have now gone from being a carbohydrate-burning machine to a fat-burning machine.

When you are burning the body's stored fat, you are losing weight. To use the correct terminology, you are in 'ketosis' or as I prefer to refer to it, you are 'fat burning'.

Over the years the biggest criticism of this diet has been that ketosis is dangerous and should be avoided. An article in the *New York Times* mentions that obesity experts are now finding it difficult to ignore the copious anecdotal evidence that this diet does just what it claims and that the medical community and the media confuse ketosis with ketoacidosis—a variant of ketosis that occurs in untreated diabetics and can be fatal.

Simply put, ketosis is evolution's answer to the thrifty gene: we may have evolved to efficiently store fat for times of famine, but we also evolved ketosis to efficiently live off that fat when necessary—rather than doing harm they make the body run more efficiently.

Being on a 'ketogenic' diet means that insulin falls so low that you enter a state of ketosis, which is what happens during fasting and starvation. Your muscles and tissues burn body fat for energy, as does your brain, in the form of fat molecules produced by the liver called ketones.

It is extremely important not to break the 'fat burning' cycle. If you take the smallest amount of sugar—just the lolly on the outside of chewing gum will do it—the 'fat burning' will cease and may take up to 48 hours before it begins again. If your body is forever in and out of 'fat burning' mode, you are going nowhere fast. Ketostix® (to test ketone levels in your urine) are available from pharmacies and will show whether or not you are fat burning. Test in the afternoon or evening for best results. You want the Ketostix® to show moderate to large. Always be aware that some medications may affect the result of the Ketostix®, however weight loss can still be achieved.

The Diet

For those of you wanting to lose weight, the first thing you need to do is determine how many g of carbohydrate you can consume to achieve 'fat burning'. I have designed the following scale to help you determine your daily carbohydrate allowance.

AMOUNT OF WEIGHT TO LOSE	GRAMS OF CARBOHYDRATES
5 to 10 kilos	10-15g per day
10 to 20 kilos	15-18g per day
20 to 40 kilos	18-25g per day
40 to 50 kilos	20-30g per day

This is the introductory period and you should follow this strictly for two weeks. This means you can eat unlimited amounts of protein but you must add up your g of carbohydrate to stay within the count. Otherwise 'fat burning' will not take place. Remember, this is totally different to anything you've ever done before. You need to forget anything you've ever done in the past—forget the kj count, forget the fat count—you are only concerned with carbohydrates.

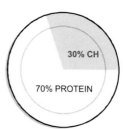

30% CH

70% PROTEIN

The Healthy Weight Range

For men and women based on Body Mass Index 20-25 BMI calculated by weight (kg) divided by Height (m)2

Height	INCHES	CENTIMETRES	KILOGRAMS
	4'7"	140	39-49
	4'8"	142	40-50
	4'9"	145	42-52
	4'10"	149	44-55
	4'11"	150	45-56
	5'0"	152	46-58
	5'1"	155	48-60
	5'2"	158	50-62
	5'3"	160	51-64
	5'4"	162	52-66
	5'5"	165	54-68
	5'6"	168	56-71
	5'7"	170	58-72
	5'8"	173	59-74
	5'9"	175	61-76
	5'10"	178	63-79
	5'11"	180	65-81
	6'0"	183	66-83
	6'1"	185	68-85
	6'2"	188	71-88

Rules:

1. You must not exceed your daily allowance of carbohydrate.

2. Eat plenty of protein. If you are hungry, you need to eat more protein.

3. A good guide is the protein 70%-carbo 30% ratio. This may take some time to get used to, as it is the opposite of what most of us were brought up with. So this is your plate.

4. Always drink at least 8-10 glasses of water (2 litres) per day—more is better.

5. Eat only from the listed foods during the first 14-day period.

6. No flour, no sugar, no bread, no fruit, no processed foods, no foods that contain 'fillers' (sausages, salami etc), no pasta or rice.

7. Do not assume that because food is classed as 'diet' food that it will be acceptable. Most 'diet' foods are low in fat but contain carbohydrate.

8. When a food is listed as containing 'no sugar', it doesn't always mean it contains no carbohydrate. Always read the label to check the CARBOHYDRATE count of foods.

9. Some foods are classed as 'carbohydrate modified'. Once again check the label.

10. Do not use sauces. These are very high in carbohydrate, most of which are hidden. These hidden carbohydrates will put your body out of 'fat burning' mode.

A GUIDE TO A STANDARD DAY
DURING THE INTRODUCTORY 14 DAY PLAN

Breakfast:

Any of the following foods are permitted (because they are protein):

- Bacon
- Ham
- Steak
- Chicken
- Fish (not cooked in bread crumbs or batter). Any amount.
- Eggs—poached, scrambled, boiled or fried. Any amount.

Lunch & Dinner:

- Meat
- Poultry
- Seafood (no bread crumbs or batter). Any amount.
- Vegetables or salad (refer to carbohydrate count list)

From the list you may choose whatever vegetables and salad you feel like and just add up the appropriate numbers to stay under your individual count for the day.

If you are hungry between meals try to snack on protein. Remember protein has no carbohydrate count. Hard-boiled eggs, chicken wings/legs, sliced ham or turkey are all acceptable. It may seem odd to begin with but remember this is not a calorie-controlled diet—it works totally differently. It's carbohydrate numbers that we are interested in only. Keep remembering the ratio of 70% protein to 30% carbohydrate.

If you are looking for something sweet—a low cal (diet) jelly is great and you can eat several during the day if you need to, as they have virtually no carbohydrate count.

Proteins

The following foods are protein and may be eaten in unlimited amounts:

- Bacon
- Beef (all cuts)
- Chicken
- Turkey
- Duck
- Pork (all cuts)
- Lamb (all cuts)
- Fish (all types)
- Eggs
- Lobster
- Mussels
- Oysters
- Prawns
- Scallops
- Shrimp
- Veal

Note: Even though these protein foods are unlimited, do not overeat or under eat. You will soon realise your level of protein.

Do not feel guilty eating your cooked breakfast. It is not so long ago that cooked breakfasts of bacon and eggs were the accepted thing. It is only more recently that we have changed our ways and taken to eating high carbohydrate breakfasts like cereal and toast, we then wonder why 1 or 2 hours after eating a high carbohydrate breakfast, we are hungry again. The fact is carbohydrates make you hungry. Protein fills you up and prevents cravings.

Vegetables

The following are a list of preferred vegetables for you to choose from in the initial stage, together with their appropriate carbohydrate counts in grams.

You choose your protein from the list and then add your vegetables or salad, being very careful to choose only the allowable amount of carbohydrate to suit your weight loss.

Also remember the ratio of 70% and 30%.

		Carbohydrate Grams
Asparagus	3 spears	2
Beans	½ cup (green)	3
Broccoli	½ cup (raw)	3
Cabbage	½ cup (cooked)	4
Carrot	1 small	5*
Celery	15cm stick (1)	1
Cucumber	4 slices	2
Capsicum	1 medium	3
Cauliflower	½ cup (raw)	3
Lettuce	2 leaves	1
Mushrooms	½ cup	1
Olives	3 medium	1
Onion	1 medium	6
Parsley	1 bunch	0
Radish	2 small	1
Shallots	1 only	1

Snow peas	30 grams	1
Spinach	½ cup (100g)	1
Tomato	1 small	3*
Zucchini	1 small (100g)	2

These are naturally high in sugar so be very aware not to exceed your limit.
You will note there are no potatoes, pumpkin, corn or peas.

Dairy Products

During the introductory period of the diet, it is wise to keep dairy products to a minimum. Even though the carbohydrate count of dairy food is not particularly high, they can slow weight loss. Dairy is lactose and turns to lactase inside your body ie. carbohydrate. Do not exceed the following allowance per day:

Hard cheese (not low fat)	25 grams
Cottage cheese	25 grams
Cream (pure)	25 ml

Low fat has a slightly higher carbohydrate count, so enjoy a little tasty cheese. Allow one gram of carbohydrate for each of the above. Only eat that amount daily.

Caffeine

Tea and coffee. Black would be best. If you must have dairy in tea or coffee, cream would be the best choice. Once again 1 teaspoon of cream should be sufficient. Remember 25 ml of cream is your daily limit.

Note: Very high consumption of caffeine may slow the fat-burning process.

Water

Most of us know that 6 to 8 glasses is the required amount of water to drink each day. Your weight loss will be a lot faster if more water is consumed. It always amazes me how much money we spend on expensive moisturisers and creams when water is the best moisturiser of all. Not only will your weight loss increase, your skin will look and feel much softer.

Sweeteners

If you normally take sugar in your tea and coffee, you will need to find a substitute. There are plenty on the market. It would be best to choose one that does not contain aspartame. Remember, the smallest amount of sugar will stop the fat burning process.

  Stevia is a good sugar replacement and is a natural herb extract from the leaf of Stevia that doesn't have any harmful chemicals present. Stevia is available in most health stores and some pharmacies.

Alcohol

Moderate use is always recommended. The following guidelines should be used while on the program.

- Scotch, bourbon, gin, vodka, brandy, rum (all are allowed as they contain only trace carbohydrate).
- Wine: only DRY white wine and red are permitted. Sweet wine contains carbohydrate.
- No beer or liqueurs.

You may use a low calorie mixer such as Diet Coke. Do not use post-mix diet soft drinks served in hotels.

  If you enjoy drinking alcohol socially, you may continue to do so. Just remember that you will lose weight faster without it. However, if you are going to resume drinking when you reach your goal weight, you are better to continue in moderation while losing weight. It is better to have a slightly slower weight loss than start old habits at your goal weight and immediately put weight on again. A moderate amount would be 3-4 drinks per week.

Salt

Salt is still a matter of contention. My advice is to listen to your body. Once again, moderation is the key. Use salt sparingly. Lite Salt is best.

Mayonnaise & Dressing

The mayonnaise and dressings we recommend are in the recipe section but for those of us who are always looking for the 'quick buy' from the supermarket, choose one that has no sugar and is very low in carbohydrate. It is important to read labels—you will be looking for carbohydrate counts not fat or kilojoules. The carbohydrate count has to come out of your daily allowance. Egg-based mayonnaise is best. Norganic Golden Soy Mayonnaise is a good buy with no sugar and no carbohydrate and is available in most supermarkets.

Fat

I personally do not believe fat is quite the bad guy it has been portrayed as and while on this diet you should choose pure fat (using butter in preference to margarine, olive oil and cooking sprays are best). It is, of course, important to choose lean cuts of meat, trim any excess fat from meats and do not add any extra fat. Even though we are only looking at carbohydrate counts in foods, we do not advocate a 'fatty diet'.

Constipation

As with any change from your normal eating patterns, you may experience some changes in bowel activity. After a short time your body will adjust but in the meantime a natural laxative may be used. Always check that there is no carbohydrate present in your choice of laxative. Plenty of water and exercise are good solutions.

Exercise

There it is in bold print. You thought you were going to avoid it. Not so. We all need some form of exercise. Depending on your current weight you might like to lose 5 to 10 kilos first and when you are feeling more comfortable, begin some form of exercise. Do not begin an exercise program you cannot maintain. Work out a realistic program, set yourself achievable goals and go after them. If a 20 minute walk three times per week is something you can achieve and maintain then great! This is better than going crazy for six weeks and then never doing it again. Exercise will enhance your weight loss and will give you more energy. You can still lose weight without exercise but you will not achieve total health and well-being. To be fit and healthy, you have to move your body. Exercise enhances bone growth, bone density and strength.

Nutritional Supplements

These are your 'edge', your 'secrets to success'. None of us live in the 'perfect' environment and for optimum health and well being especially while attempting to lose weight—nutritional supplements are essential.

The following is a list of the 'most essential':

- Vitamin B
- Vitamin C
- Calcium
- Potassium
- Zinc

At the very least you should take a good multi-vitamin. If money is not too much of a consideration, or you have access to organic food, I would certainly recommend it but do understand that it can sometimes be beyond the family budget—long term though the health benefits could be well worth it.

Overview

For the first three to four days on the plan, some people may feel unwell. You may actually feel quite nauseous and experience headaches. Particularly if your carbohydrate intake has been high. What you are experiencing is 'carbohydrate withdrawal'. If it persists, you may add 2 slices of tomato to your breakfast or have half an apple mid morning, just until your body adjusts. And it will. A week later, you will be feeling so good you won't believe everybody doesn't eat this way. Some people may find taking chromium tablets helpful as they help to stabilise blood sugar levels.

If you want to give up tea and coffee, by all means do so, but SLOWLY. Caffeine withdrawal and carbohydrate withdrawal can make you feel very unwell. Not to mention BIG HEADACHES.

A good way to reduce caffeine intake is to substitute every second cup with decaffeinated products or ¼ teaspoon decaf to ¾ teaspoon regular coffee in each cup. Then ½ and ½, eventually weaning yourself off caffeine completely. Be kind to yourself and make the changes slowly.

FOOD SUGGESTIONS FOR INITIAL TWO WEEK PERIOD

Breakfast:

Bacon

Bacon and Eggs

Eggs Fried

Eggs Poached

Eggs Boiled

Eggs Scrambled (no milk) add teaspoon cream and tbsp water

Omelette (no milk) add tbsp water

Ham

Ham and Eggs

Ham topped with 25g cheese

Lunch:

Ham Slices with	4 slices cucumber
	½ tomato 1 slice cheese (25g)
Chicken Pieces with	3 asparagus spears
	2 slices tomato
	2 lettuce leaves
Tuna (unflavoured) with	1 boiled egg
	2 slices cucumber
	2 lettuce leaves
Boiled Eggs with	1 slice cheese (25g)
	2 slices tomato
	1 stick celery
	3 medium olives
Roast Beef/Lamb/Pork with	2 lettuce leaves
	¼ cup cabbage (shredded)
	½ small carrot (shredded)
	2 slices tomato
Salmon with	2 lettuce leaves
	1 slice cheese (25g)
	3 asparagus spears
	4 slices cucumber
Meat Balls with	2 lettuce leaves
	½ tomato

Bind meat balls with egg only—no flour.

Prawns	2 lettuce leaves
	2 slices tomato, 4 slices cucumber
Fish (no breadcrumbs or batter) with	
	½ small carrot (shredded)
	¼ cup cabbage (shredded)
	2 slices capsicum
	2 slices tomato

Dinner:

Steak with

½ cup cauliflower
½ cup green beans
½ cup mushrooms (may be cooked in butter)

Fish (grilled or
panfried) with

½ cup broccoli
½ small carrot
½ cup cauliflower
or
2 slices tomato
2 lettuce leaves
4 slices cucumber
2 slices onion

Roast Chicken with

½ cup cauliflower
½ cup spinach
½ cup green beans
½ small carrot

Roast Lamb/Beef with

½ tomato stewed
½ medium onion (stewed)
½ cup cauliflower
¼ cup green beans

Prawns/Lobster with

2 lettuce leaves
½ tomato
4 slices cucumber
¼ cup cabbage (shredded)
½ small carrot (shredded)

Snacks:

Boiled Eggs
Sliced Ham or any meat
Meat Balls
Low Cal Jelly
Pork Krackles
Atkins Snack Bars
10 Almonds
Sugar Free Lollies
Cadbury Lite Chocolate (3 squares per day only)
Prawns, Mussels, Oysters
Amaretti Biscuits.

Supermarket Shopping

• Pork Krackles are available in most supermarkets in the nuts and chips section.

• Atkins Morning Shine Bars and Atkins Advantage Bars are located in the vitamin section of Woolworths supermarkets.

• Sugar Free Lollies, eg., DD's; Ricci Lite n Luscious; Jol's Sugar Free Pastilles; Extra Chewing Gum; Smint Lollies; Zones Drops; are all fine to use on the diet but be very aware that excessive consumption may have a laxative effect. Always check the carbohydrate count and allow for it in your daily allowance.

• Amaretti Almond Macaroon Biscuits available most supermarkets 2.4g per serve.

• Woolworths Lean Aussie Burger 100% Beef 0g carbohydrates.

• Sausages: Beef Chavapi (Woolworths) —.25g carbohydrates per sausage. Coles Italian or Coles Chilli Italian—1gm carbohydrate per sausage.

Slow Weight Loss

This can be caused by any number of things from fluid retention to changes in medication or just being pre-menstrual, but here are a couple of things to check for:

Dairy—Have you exceeded your daily limit? Have you started just pouring the cream into your coffee instead of measuring it?

Have you started using milk again?

Has your cheese increased?

Are you still carefully adding up your g of carbohydrate or have you started guessing? (you'll go over)

Are you checking for Ketosis?

Has sugar crept in anywhere?

Have you increased your caffeine intake?

How much alcohol are you consuming?

If you have made a few errors, so what, it just proves you are quite normal—now it's time to get back on track—remember you won't continue to lose every week in the same amounts as you did initially.

Also remember ½ kilo a week is a nice steady weight loss. If you are old enough to remember stones and pounds, you will remember that if you lost a pound (less than ½ a kilo) a week it was good. Now everyone thinks they should lose a kilo a week—yet, nothing else has changed, except we went metric. Just remember losing weight is never easy—it's one of the hardest things to do or there wouldn't be hundreds of books on the subject—Jenny Craig and all the other (too numerous to mention) Weight Loss Clinics wouldn't be around. Just try to take it one day at a time. Reward yourself when you succeed (not with food) and shrug your shoulders when you fall by the wayside. Try to drink a little extra water—put out a bit more exercise—and just get on with it.

Success at losing weight is directly proportionate to your personal commitment, determination and enthusiasm. Make it an enjoyable experience.

After the Introductory Two Weeks

Some of you with only a few kilos to lose may very well have achieved your goal weight already. If so, congratulations and you should move on to the maintenance section.

For those who wish to lose more weight, you can continue but you may now make use of the delicious recipes in the recipe section.

You may also increase your carbohydrate count by 5g and monitor your weight loss weekly. If no loss, cut back the extra 5 grams.

It would be best if you could weigh once a week, preferably on the same day each week, and at about the same time and in the same clothes. If you are continuing to lose you may increase another 5g of carbohydrate and continue to monitor your loss.

Remember to use the Ketostix® , as they will tell you if you are still in 'fat burning' mode. You can then tell if you need to decrease or to stay on the same carbohydrate level. Every person has his or her own carbohydrate level where 'fat burning' will cease. To find your own level use the Ketostix®.

As we are all individuals with differing metabolisms, no two people are the same. Once you find your carbohydrate level where you can continue to lose weight, you can eat any of the foods from the lists and from the recipes. Just keep adding the g of carbohydrates to stay within your level. You are still best to leave out fruit until you start maintenance or if you introduce them, use the very low carbohydrate fruit such as strawberries.

Maintenance

Congratulations—you should be looking and feeling like a new person.

Now comes the challenge of keeping your weight off.

If you have enjoyed eating this way and want to continue to enjoy the benefits this method of eating provides, then you should slowly start to increase your carbohydrateg until you find your maintenance level.

Fruit would be the first thing to introduce and then more vegetables.

Some of you will find that you will maintain on 30g of carbohydrate per day while others can take in 60 grams. You will find that you can have your little splurges and by getting back on track straight away you will do no damage.

Try to set yourself a goal weight with a base weight and a ceiling. For example: you may say you don't want to ever go over 60kg, so for you 58kg is your base weight and 60kg is your ceiling. You should ideally float between 58kg and 60kg. That way you can have a weekend away and lash out. If you go over your ceiling weight then you need to go back to the introductory program again for 1 or 2 weeks to get back to your goal weight. When you have reached your goal weight then go back to the maintenance plan. Try not to exceed your daily maintenance carbohydrate count.

Note: Once on maintenance, your body should not be in ketosis.

Benefits

A lot of you may have already noticed how good you feel. Most people will enjoy better health, lowered blood sugar levels, lowered cholesterol and triglycerides.

Something else, which is no small thing, is that people continually make comment on the fact that you do not get the usual 'pinched' or 'gaunt' look that is associated with weight loss. People on low fat or low kilojoule diet plans often get this look and their skin becomes dry and pale and lines appear.

With a low carbohydrate/high protein diet, there is more essential fatty acid in the food, therefore the skin looks better and is more supple and less prone to the aging effect.

You now have all the essential information you need to lose your weight, maintain it and enjoy renewed energy and better health without all the technical jargon that can be so confusing.

BREAKFAST

Breakfast Stack

Ingredients

2 bacon rashers
1 egg
10g hard cheese
1 slice tomato

Carbs 1g
per serve

Method

Cook bacon under grill. Spray egg ring with oil.
Cook egg until firm. Assemble stack by placing cooked egg on serving plate. Bacon next, then tomato. Top with cheese. Place stack under grill for approximately 2 minutes.

Cheesy Eggs in the Pan

serves 1

Ingredients

2 eggs
30g tasty hard cheese

Carbs 1g
per serve

Method

Melt butter in pan. Place eggs in pan and cook until whites begin to set. Add cheese on top of egg. Cook approximately 1 minute, turn and continue to cook until cheese is golden brown.

Light Curried Eggs

Ingredients

4 eggs
½ teaspoon curry powder
2 tablespoons butter
½ teaspoon finely chopped garlic
½ teaspoon finely chopped parsley

Method

Sauté garlic in butter until soft, approximately 8 minutes. Add curry powder. Stir well. Beat eggs lightly. Stir into garlic mixture and cook over low heat, stirring occasionally until eggs are set. Sprinkle parsley into egg mixture just before taking from pan. Can be served in lettuce cups.

Creamy Cheese Baked Eggs

Ingredients

4 eggs
¼ cup heavy cream
Grated Parmesan cheese
Cracked black pepper to taste and salt
1 tablespoon butter
4 tablespoons grated hard cheese

Method

Preheat oven to 180°C. Butter four custard cups or small ramekins. Break an egg carefully into each cup. Sprinkle with salt and pepper. Spoon 1 tablespoon of cream over each egg. Bake for approximately 8 minutes. Add 1 tablespoon of grated cheese and Parmesan cheese. Return to oven for further 2 minutes.

Gourmet Egg Delight

Ingredients

1 packet frozen spinach
¼ cup grated parmesan cheese
4 eggs
4 tablespoons cream
Grated nutmeg
Cracked black pepper
Butter

Method

Cook spinach according to directions on packet. Drain well and place in buttered ramekin dishes (4). Make indentation and break egg into each. Top with grated cheese, cream and cracked pepper. Bake in preheated moderate oven (180°C) for approximately 15 minutes or until eggs are set.

Basic Omelette

Ingredients

2 eggs
1 tablespoon shallots
1 teaspoon chopped parsley
1 tablespoon heavy cream
Salt and pepper to taste

Method

Combine all ingredients and beat lightly.
Spray non-stick pan. Pour egg mixture into pan.
Cook without stirring, 1-2 minutes, carefully flip one side onto the other side to form semi-circle. Slide onto plate and serve.

Cheese Pancakes

Ingredients

1 cup cottage cheese
6 eggs
3 tablespoons soy protein isolate (or soy flour)
3 tablespoons melted butter
Pinch salt

Method

Blend all ingredients in blender until smooth.
Heat pan until very hot—spray pan and drop a teaspoon of batter onto the pan and brown on both sides.

Ham Slice

Ingredients

1 slice ham, approx 3mm thick
1 teaspoon dry mustard
½ cup heavy cream
¼ cup grated hard cheese

Method

Place ham on the grill rack under preheated grill and cook until ham is brown. Turn and spread with mixture of mustard and cream and return to the griller until topping is bubbling. Sprinkle with grated cheese and grill until cheese is melted.

Asparagus Omelette

serves 4

Carbs 5g
per serve

Ingredients

16 sticks asparagus
2 tablespoons butter
8 eggs
Salt and pepper to taste
Paprika

Method

Cut asparagus into 2cm pieces. Melt butter in pan. Add asparagus and cook on medium heat until heated through. Beat eggs with salt and pepper and pour into pan. Cover and cook until eggs are set. Remove and place on platter, garnishing with paprika.

Hearty Breakfast Treat

Ingredients

2 eggs
3 bacon rashers
2 slices tomato (thin)
½ cup mushrooms (sliced)
2 tablespoons butter
Oil spray

Method

Spray hot frying pan with oil. Break eggs into pan and cook to desired consistency (hard or soft centres). Remove eggs from pan and keep hot. Place butter in pan and fry bacon. Cook 1-2 minutes. Add mushrooms and tomato to pan and cook until mushrooms are soft and tomato brown. Place eggs and contents of pan onto serving dish and serve immediately.

Quick Breakfast Cups (microwave)

Ingredients

2 eggs
¼ cup chopped bacon
¼ cup chopped shallots
¼ cup grated tasty cheese
¼ cup grated carrot
Oil spray

Method

Combine all ingredients with a whisk. Spray four small microwave safe dishes with oil. Spoon mixture into each dish. Microwave uncovered, on HIGH power for 1-1½ minutes or until set. Stand for 5 minutes before turning out onto serving dish. Serve immediately.

Breakfast Pick Me Up

serves 4

Carbs 2g
per serve

Ingredients

2 cups of hot water
4 tablespoons whey powder
1 raw egg
10 medium strawberries
1 tablespoon yoghurt

Method

Blend all ingredients together. Serve immediately.

Creamy Scrambled Eggs

serves 1

Carbs 1.6g
per serve

Helpful Hint
• When making
scrambled eggs,
omelettes etc.
water can be
substituted
instead of milk as
it gives a lighter
texture.

Ingredients

2 eggs
1 tablespoon cream
1 tablespoon butter
1 tablespoon chopped parsley
Salt and pepper to taste

Method

Combine eggs and cream and beat well with a whisk. Melt butter in a non stick frying pan. Add egg mixture and cook on a low heat until eggs are set. Add parsley, salt and pepper. When mixture is set scramble with a fork. Spoon into a serving dish. Serve immediately.

Herb Pancakes

Ingredients

1 cup cottage cheese

6 eggs

3 tablespoons soy flour

3 tablespoons butter (melted)

1 tablespoon chopped parsley

1 tablespoon chopped chives

1 teaspoon salt

Oil spray

Method

Place all ingredients in a blender. Blend until smooth. Spray a non stick frying pan with oil. Heat pan until very hot. Drop tablespoons of batter into pan. Brown pancakes on both sides. Serve hot.

Sweet Omelette

Ingredients

1 cup soft cream cheese

8 eggs

¼ cup cream

2 tablespoons sugar substitute

2 tablespoons butter

1 cup chopped strawberries

Method

Combine cheese, eggs, cream and sugar in a bowl and beat until smooth. Cook the omelette following the Basic Omelette recipe (page 33). When the centre of the omelette is firm, spoon the strawberries on to the centre and fold in half. Slide on to serving dish and serve immediately.

Vegetarian Omelette

Ingredients

2 eggs
½ teaspoon butter
¼ cup mixed frozen vegetables (thawed)
¼ cup grated cheese
¼ cup cream
¼ teaspoon curry powder
Freshly ground black pepper

Method

Beat eggs, cream, pepper and curry powder together until frothy. Heat non-stick frying pan or omelette pan. Melt butter making sure bottom of pan is covered. Add egg mixture and cook on medium heat until mixture is set. Add vegetables and grated cheese to one half then carefully fold other half on top. Cook for a further one minute. Slide omelette onto a serving dish and serve immediately.

SNACKS & LIGHT MEALS

Vegetable Chop Suey

serves 4

Carbs 8g
per serve

Ingredients

1 red capsicum

1 yellow capsicum

1 carrot

1 zucchini

1 onion

60g snow peas

2 tablespoons oil

3 garlic cloves (crushed)

1 teaspoon grated fresh ginger

125g bean sprouts

2 tablespoons light soy sauce

½ cup vegetable stock

Method

Cut capsicums, carrot and zucchini into thin slices. Cut onion into quarters and then cut each quarter in half. Slice snow peas diagonally. Make sure that the vegetables are all cut into pieces of a similar size so they cook within the same amount of time. Heat the oil in a preheated wok, add garlic and stir fry for 30 seconds. Add onion and stir fry for a further 30 seconds. Add capsicums, carrot, zucchini and snow peas to the wok and stir fry for 2 minutes. Add the bean sprouts to the wok and stir in the soy sauce and stock. Reduce heat to low and simmer for 1-2 minutes until the vegetables are tender and coated with the sauce. Transfer the vegetables and sauce to a serving dish and serve immediately.

Crabmeat Patties

Ingredients

225g crabmeat, drained and flaked
1 garlic clove, crushed
½ cup parmesan cheese, grated
½ teaspoon finely chopped parsley
1 egg
Salt and pepper to taste

Method

Combine crabmeat, garlic, cheese, parsley, egg, salt and pepper into a mixing bowl and form into small balls. Heat oil in a pan and fry each side until golden brown.

Savoury Omelette

Ingredients

8 lean bacon rashers
1 large onion chopped (1 cup)
8 eggs

2 tablespoons cream
½ teaspoon salt
Freshly ground black pepper to taste

Method

Cut bacon into small pieces and fry in a non-stick pan until crisp. Add onion and cook until transparent. Pour off all fat. Set aside until omelette is ready. Follow basic omelette recipe (above) using half egg mixture. When cooked, place half the bacon and egg in the centre of the omelette before folding over. Then, fold over and cook for a further minute. Move to a serving plate and cover to keep warm. Make the second omelette the same way. Cut each omelette in half and serve immediately.

Simple Onion & Garlic Dip

Ingredients

2 tablespoons chopped onion
2 tablespoons olive oil
1 cup sour cream
1 clove garlic (crushed)
½ teaspoon chopped parsley

Method

In a small frying pan, fry onion and garlic in olive oil until onion is deep brown. Remove from heat and let cool. When completely cooled, add to sour cream. Stir well to ensure complete mixture of onions, garlic, oil and sour cream. Before serving add in chopped parsley. Serve on cucumber slices or in celery stalks.

Chicken Drumsticks

Ingredients

1kg chicken drumsticks
1 cup soy sauce
2 tablespoons oil
2 cloves garlic (crushed)
Artificial sweetener

Pinch paprika
Pinch cumin
Pinch coriander
Pinch allspice
Salt and pepper to taste

Method

Combine all ingredients in a marinade and refrigerate for 1½ hours. Preheat oven to 180°C. Bake in marinade for 20-30 minutes or until chicken is cooked. Baste chicken frequently while cooking.

serves 2

Carbs 2g
per slice

* Soy
protein
available in
most health
food stores.

Sundried Tomato Loaf

Ingredients

6 eggs
¼ cup pure soy protein*
½ teaspoon cream of tartare
½ cup chopped sundried tomatoes

1 teaspoon chopped basil
1 teaspoon sugar substitute
¼ cup almond meal

Method

Separate eggs and place whites and yolks in two large bowls. Beat egg whites, cream of tartare and sugar substitute until stiff peaks form. Beat yolks then add soy protein, almond meal and basil and mix well. Add enough whites to yolk mixture to make batter. Fold yolk mixture into remaining whites. Blend well. Add sundried tomatoes, spoon batter into well greased 20cm loaf pan. Bake at 180°C for 30-40 minutes, turning after 15 minutes. When cool, slice into 12 pieces.

Marinated Chicken Livers

Ingredients

6 chicken livers, cut in half
6 slices bacon, cut in half
½ cup dry sherry
3 tablespoons unsweetened pineapple juice
1 tablespoon fresh ginger, minced
1 tablespoon soy sauce

Method

Combine sherry, juice, ginger and soy sauce.
Add chicken livers and marinate in the fridge for 2 hours. Preheat oven to 180°C. Wrap each chicken liver with a piece of bacon and secure with a toothpick through centre. Place the chicken livers on a non-stick tray and bake for 10-15 minutes until bacon is cooked through.

Light Easy Omelette

Ingredients

½ cup grated zucchini
½ cup button mushrooms (sliced)
1 egg white

1 whole egg (separated)
1 tablespoon cream
1 tablespoon grated hard cheese
Spray oil

Method

Spray hot omelette pan or frying pan with oil. Sauté mushrooms. Toss through zucchini to heat. Remove vegetables from pan and keep warm. Beat egg white in a clean, dry bowl with electric hand beater or whisk until peaks form. Mix in yolk and cream. Lightly spray pan with oil again. Pour mixture into pan. Cook for 2-3 minutes or until base is golden and firm. Place under hot grill for approximately 1 minute to cook top of the omelette. Do not overcook. Top with mushroom mixture. Sprinkle with cheese. Fold in half and serve immediately.

Chinese Omelette

Ingredients

8 eggs
225g cooked chicken meat, shredded
12 medium sized tiger prawns, peeled
and chopped into bite sized pieces

2 tablespoons chopped chives
2 teaspoons light soy sauce
2 tablespoons vegetable oil

Method

Lightly beat the eggs in a large bowl. Add the shredded chicken and prawns to the eggs and mix well. Stir in chopped chives and light soy sauce and combine well. Heat the vegetable oil in a large preheated frying pan over a medium heat, gently stirring the omelette with a fork until the surface is just set and the underside is a golden brown colour. When the omelette is set, slide it out of the pan with the aid of a spatula. Cut omelette into slices and serve immediately.

Cheesy Spinach Slice

serves 4

Carbs 2g
per serve

Ingredients

350g frozen chopped spinach
100g cottage cheese
6 eggs (lightly beaten)
½ cup grated mild cheese
¼ cup melted butter
¼ teaspoon nutmeg
¼ teaspoon cracked black pepper

Method

Preheat oven to 180°C. Thaw and drain spinach, squeezing out any excess liquid. Lightly grease a casserole dish or suitable baking dish. In a mixing bowl, blend together spinach, cottage cheese, butter, eggs, grated cheese, nutmeg and pepper. Pour mixture into baking dish. Cook for 1 hour.

Crunchy Avocado Salad

Ingredients

200g mixed green salad leaves

3 shallots

3 tablespoons fresh chopped coriander

2 red capsicums

1 large avocado

1 tablespoon lime juice

3-4 tablespoons pumpkin seeds (toasted)

Dressing

Juice of 1 lime

¼ teaspoon paprika

¼ teaspoon ground cumin

1¼ teaspoon sugar substitute

4 tablespoons extra virgin olive oil

1 clove garlic (crushed)

Method

Combine the salad leaves with shallots and coriander. Toss together then transfer the salad to a large serving dish. Slice capsicum thinly. Add to salad leaves. Cut avocado in half. Carefully peel off the skin, dice the flesh and toss in the lime juice to prevent the avocado discolouring. Add to the other salad ingredients.

Dressing

Whisk together the lime juice, paprika, ground cumin, sugar substitute, garlic and olive oil. Pour the dressing over the salad and toss lightly. Sprinkle with the toasted pumpkin seeds.

*Crunchy
Avocado
Salad*

*Caesar
Salad*

Caesar Salad

Ingredients

4 rashers bacon
8 tablespoons parmesan cheese (grated)
4 hard-boiled eggs (sliced lengthways)
4 Cos lettuce leaves (broken)
6 tablespoons thickened cream

2 tablespoons lemon juice
2 cloves garlic (crushed)
Black pepper to taste
1 tablespoon Worcestershire sauce

Method

Grill the bacon until crisp. Chop into bite sized pieces. Toss bacon with parmesan cheese, eggs and lettuce. Combine thoroughly. Place cream, lemon juice, garlic, black pepper, Worcestershire sauce in jar. Screw on lid and shake well. Pour dressing over salad. Serve immediately.

Ham Pizza Slices

Ingredients

4 ham steaks
4 slices cheese
½ large onion (sliced)
2 tablespoons tomato paste

Method

Spread tomato paste over each ham steak. Then separate sliced onion into 4 serves, spread over tomato paste then place cheese on top. Grill for 3-4 minutes until cheese melts and bubbles.

Mushroom Frittata

Ingredients

1½ cups mushrooms (coarsely chopped)
4 spring onions
4 tablespoons butter
salt to taste
6 eggs
2 tablespoons cream
½ teaspoon curry powder

Method

Sauté onions and mushrooms in olive oil until browned. Add salt and curry powder. Beat eggs with cream. Pour over onion and mushroom mixture and keep on a low heat. Frittata is cooked when mixture is set. Serve immediately.

Vegetable Frittata

Ingredients

8 eggs (beaten lightly)
2 cups pumpkin (coarsely chopped)
1 cup cauliflower (coarsely chopped)

1 cup zucchini (grated)
200g feta cheese (crumbled)
¾ cup cheddar cheese (coarsely grated)
1 small onion (sliced thinly into rings)

Method

Preheat oven to very hot. Grease deep 23cm square cake pan, line base and side with baking paper. Boil or steam pumpkin and cauliflower. Combine pumpkin and cauliflower in a large bowl then add zucchini, cheese and egg. Stir to combine. Transfer mixture into prepared pan and top with onion rings. Bake in hot oven for approximately 25 minutes or until firm. Allow to stand for 5 minutes before serving.

Helpful Hint
• Mushrooms are best stored unwashed in brown paper bags. In the fridge the lowest shelf is the best place for mushrooms as the air flow is slightly better than the crisper section.

SOUPS

Prawn Soup

Ingredients

1kg prawns—peeled
6 cups homemade chicken stock
(see page 142)
2 tablespoons olive oil
3 cloves garlic
5 celery stalks
2 green peppers—diced
6 tablespoons mayonnaise
½ teaspoon paprika
½ teaspoon oregano
½ teaspoon thyme
Salt and pepper to taste
¼ cup fresh minced parsley

Method

Heat oil in pan. Add celery, garlic and pepper and sauté until softened. Add mayonnaise and spices and sauté approximately 1½ minutes. Add chicken stock. Cover and cook on medium heat about 35 minutes or until thickened. Add prawns and simmer five minutes. Season with salt and pepper.

Bacon & Cauliflower Soup

serves 2

Carbs 6.5g
per serve

Ingredients

2 tablespoons butter
2 cups cauliflower pieces
1 cup bacon bits
2 tablespoons lemon juice
1 cup homemade chicken stock (see Dips and Stocks)
black pepper
½ cup cream
parsley to garnish

Method

Melt the butter and cook cauliflower and bacon for 5 minutes. Add lemon juice, stock and pepper. Simmer until cauliflower is tender. Puree until smooth and add cream. Heat slowly and garnish with chopped parsley.

Meat & Vegie Soup

serves 4

Carbs 5g
per serve

Ingredients

Lamb shanks (any amount)
2 tablespoons oil
3 bay leaves
1 large onion, diced
2 cups cabbage
3 sticks celery, sliced
1 cup spinach (shredded)

1 cup broccoli pieces
1 cup sliced green beans
2 litres beef stock
1 cup bacon bits
2 tablespoons sugar free tomato paste
3 tablespoons peppercorns
½ cup cream

Method

Heat oil and brown shanks. Drain off fat. Cover with water, bay leaves and peppercorns. Simmer for 45 minutes or until meat is tender. Add vegetables and beef stock. Bring to boil and simmer for 15 minutes or until vegetables are tender. Add cream prior to serving and garnish with chopped parsley.

Mushroom Soup

serves 4

Carbs 4.5g
per serve

Ingredients

2 tablespoons oil
1 onion finely diced
½ clove garlic minced
1 litre chicken stock
2 tablespoons lemon juice

2 cups sliced mushrooms
2 tablespoons finely chopped parsley
Black pepper and lite salt
3 shallots finely chopped
½ cup cream

Method

Heat oil in saucepan, fry onion and garlic for 2 minutes. Add mushrooms and cook while stirring continuously until tender. Add chicken stock and simmer for 5 minutes. Add shallots, parsley, salt and pepper and bring to boil. Simmer further 10 minutes. Puree soup until smooth and add cream. Heat gently before serving. Garnish with parsley.

Bacon & Vegetable Soup

serves 2

Carbs 6g
per serve

Ingredients

½ cup cauliflower pieces
½ onion (diced)
½ cup zucchini (diced)
2 cups chicken stock
3 rashers lean bacon (diced)

Method

Place cauliflower, zucchini, stock and onion in a saucepan and cook until very soft. Puree until smooth. Dry fry the bacon until brown and add to the pureed vegetable mix. Gently heat and serve.

Thai Tangy Soup

Ingredients

10 green prawns
1 teaspoon ginger (freshly grated)
3 cups fish or vegetable stock
4 shallots (finely sliced)
2 celery sticks (thinly sliced)

1 red chilli (finely sliced)
1 garlic clove (crushed)
1 tablespoon lemon grass (finely sliced)
1 tablespoon fish sauce
½ cup mushrooms (thinly sliced)
½ cup bean sprouts

Method

Lightly spray a saucepan with cooking spray. Add the garlic and cook for 1 minute. Add the ginger, lemon grass and fish or vegetable stock and simmer for 15 minutes. Strain the stock and discard the garlic, ginger and lemon grass. Put the stock back into the saucepan and add the rest of the ingredients except the bean sprouts. Simmer until the prawns have turned a light orange colour. Serve hot with the bean sprouts on top.

Zucchini Soup

Ingredients

500g zucchini (chopped)
1 large onion (chopped)
1 teaspoon parsley (chopped)
1 teaspoon mixed herbs
1 cup chicken stock
1 cup cream
Cracked black pepper

Method

Place zucchini and onion in a large saucepan. Cover vegetables with chicken stock, herbs and seasoning. Cook until tender.

When cool, place mixture in blender and puree. Return mixture to saucepan. Add cream slowly, continuously stirring. Heat mixture through.

Add parsley and cracked pepper to taste.

Serve immediately.

Creamy Mushroom Soup

Ingredients

2 cups mushrooms (sliced)
1 small onion (finely diced)
1 garlic clove (minced)
1 cup cream
1 litre chicken stock
2 tablespoons parsley (finely chopped)
1 tablespoon butter
Cracked black pepper and salt
(to taste)

Method

Heat butter in saucepan. Sauté onions and garlic. Cook until onion has colour. Add mushrooms. Cook until mushrooms become soft. Add chicken stock and simmer for 5 minutes. Add parsley, salt and pepper to taste. Allow mixture to cool slightly. Puree soup until smooth. Return mixture to saucepan and slowly reheat. Add cream stirring continuously.

Serve immediately.

Taste of Asia

Ingredients

1 whole chicken breast (cut in half)
250g green beans (fresh, trimmed and cut in half)
1 litre chicken stock

4 shallots (sliced)
1 stick lemon grass (white only, sliced finely)
1 tablespoon ginger (minced)
2 tablespoons soy sauce

Method

Bring all ingredients, except chicken and beans to the boil, in a large saucepan. Reduce heat and simmer for 3-4 minutes. Add chicken breasts. Simmer gently for a further 7-8 minutes. Remove chicken from broth. Set aside and keep warm. Add beans to broth. Cook until beans are tender. Ladle broth and beans into Asian serving bowls. Slice chicken breasts into thin slices and place on top of each bowl. Serve immediately.

Roast Capsicum & Ginger Soup

Ingredients

1 small whole cauliflower (chopped)
2 medium onions (chopped)
2 large red capsicums (roasted, seeded and peeled)
1 teaspoon minced ginger
1 litre chicken stock
1 tablespoon butter

Method

Heat butter in a large saucepan. Sauté onions and ginger for approximately 3 minutes or until onion has softened. Add all remaining ingredients. Bring to the boil. Reduce heat. Simmer for approximately 20 minutes or until all vegetables are well cooked. Allow mixture to cool. Puree soup in a blender. Reheat to serve.

Seafood Soup

Ingredients

500g green prawns (peeled and deveined)
500g white fleshed boned fish (chopped)
1 large red capsicum (diced)
3 celery stalks (finely diced)
2 large tablespoons olive oil
½ cup cream
1½ litres chicken stock
¼ cup fresh parsley (chopped)
½ teaspoon paprika
½ teaspoon dried oregano
½ teaspoon dried thyme
2 cloves garlic
Cracked black pepper

Method

Heat olive oil in a large saucepan over medium heat. Add garlic, celery and capsicum and sauté until soft, approximately 5 minutes. Add cream, paprika, oregano and thyme and cook for a further 1 minute. Slowly add stock and bring to boil. Cook over medium-high heat for 25 minutes or until mixture has thickened. Add prawns and fish pieces and simmer until prawns are pink and fish opaque and cooked through. Season with cracked pepper to taste. Add soup to serving bowls and sprinkle with chopped parsley.

Bacon & Cauliflower Soup with Parmesan Crisps

Ingredients

1 tablespoon olive oil
1 onion (roughly chopped)
500g bacon bones (cut into pieces)
1 cauliflower
1 litre water
½ cup freshly grated parmesan
¼ cup cream (optional)
½ teaspoon horseradish cream
Salt and white pepper
1 tablespoon chives (diced)
2 bay leaves

Method

Heat the olive oil in a large heavy-based saucepan. Sauté the onion and bacon bones over the heat for 5 minutes. Add the cauliflower, water and bay leaves and bring to the boil. Reduce the heat to moderately low and simmer the soup for 15 minutes. Remove the saucepan from the heat, set aside to cool slightly. Remove and discard the bacon bones and bay leaves and process the soup in a food processor in two batches until smooth. Preheat oven to 200°C. Place tablespoons of parmesan cheese onto baking trays, spread out to form 6cm rounds, bake in batches 5-7 minutes or until crisp and golden. Working quickly, lift the parmesan crisps from the tray and set aside on a cooling rack. Return the soup to a saucepan and warm gently, add cream and horseradish and season. Sprinkle with the chives and serve with the parmesan crisps.

Home-style Tomato Soup

Ingredients

400g can tomatoes (diced)
1 medium onion (diced)
2 large garlic cloves (crushed)
1 litre chicken stock

¼ cup fresh parsley (finely chopped)
2 tablespoons olive oil
½ teaspoon cracked black pepper
1 tablespoon fresh basil

Method

Heat oil in a large saucepan. Sauté onion, garlic and tomatoes.
Cook until onion is soft, approximately 3 minutes. Add stock, parsley and pepper.
Simmer for 30 minutes. When serving place fresh basil on top of soup.

Summer Soup

Ingredients

200g fresh mushrooms, chopped
2 cups chicken consommé
1 envelope unflavoured gelatine
½ cup cold water
½ cup dry white wine
250ml plain yoghurt
Chopped parsley
Salt and pepper to taste

Method

Simmer mushrooms in chicken consommé for approximately 25 minutes. Strain. Sprinkle gelatine over water and let soften. Add to soup and stir until dissolved. Add salt and pepper and stir in wine. Chill until firm and serve individually with yoghurt topping and parsley.

VEGETARIAN

VEGETARIAN

Tomato & Mushroom Salad

serves 4

Carbs 5g
per serve

Ingredients

4 small fresh tomatoes
10 button mushrooms
Small bowl washed lettuce
2 tablespoons lemon/lime juice

Dressing
2 tablespoons virgin olive oil
½ cup fresh basil
½ teaspoon salt
½ teaspoon cracked black pepper

Method

Place lettuce in serving bowl. Cut tomatoes and mushrooms into bite sized pieces and toss through with lettuce.

Dressing

Mix together oil, lemon juice, salt, pepper and finely chopped basil. Pour over salad just before serving.

Spicy Sautéed Vegetables

Ingredients

2 medium tomatoes
(seeded and pureed)
1½ tablespoons horseradish
2 tablespoons dry red wine
½ packet sugar substitute
2 teaspoons olive oil

2 cloves garlic minced
1 teaspoon minced basil
½ teaspoon minced oregano
2 small zucchini, sliced
½ cup sliced mushrooms
½ cup cherry tomatoes, cut into halves

Method

In a bowl combine pureed tomatoes, horseradish, wine and sweetener. Heat oil in saucepan on medium heat. Add garlic and sauté for 30 seconds. Increase heat slightly and add basil and oregano and stirfry for 30 seconds. Reduce heat slightly, add zucchini and mushrooms and sauté for 2 minutes. Add tomatoes and pureed tomato mix and cook covered over med-low heat for 5 minutes. Serve with chicken.

Silver Beet & Mushroom Slice

Ingredients

2 tablespoons olive oil

2 onions (finely sliced)

3 cloves garlic (chopped)

500g mushrooms cups
(thickly sliced)

1 bunch silver beet
(roughly chopped)

Salt and freshly ground black pepper

4 eggs

300ml cream

½ cup tasty cheese (grated)

Method

Preheat oven to 180°C. Heat the olive oil in a large saucepan over a moderate heat. Sauté the onion and garlic for 5 minutes or until soft. Add the mushrooms and sauté for another 2 minutes. Add the silver beet and season. Cover the saucepan and cook until the silver beet wilts. Remove from the heat, stir the silver beet through the mushrooms and drain any excess moisture. Transfer the silver beet mixture into a large 6 cup capacity baking dish. Whisk the eggs and cream together, season and stir through the grated cheese. Pour the egg mixture over the silver beet mixture, swirl the egg mixture through the silver beet using a fork. Bake for 40 minutes or until golden and set. Allow to cool slightly before slicing.

Quick & Easy Vegetable Mix

Ingredients

500g frozen mixed vegetables

½ tablespoon minced oregano

½ cup chicken broth

1 teaspoon lemon pepper

1 tablespoon butter

Salt and pepper to taste

½ tablespoon minced basil

Method

Steam vegetables in broth until tender. Remove vegetables and reduce the liquid in pan to 2 tablespoons. Add the butter, minced basil and oregano and lemon pepper. Drizzle over vegetables and serve with your choice of meat.

Crustless Vegetable Quiche

Ingredients

1 cup carrot (grated)
1 cup zucchini (grated)
¼ cup shallots (finely chopped)

120g cheddar cheese (grated)
6 eggs
1 cup cream
Cracked black pepper and salt

Method

Preheat oven to 180°C. In a large bowl, add grated carrot, zucchini and shallots. Combine beaten eggs, cream, pepper and salt. Add egg mixture to vegetables. Stir through cheese.

Spray a 23cm quiche dish with a non-stick spray. Pour mixture into dish. Bake in a preheated moderate oven for approximately 40 minutes or until mixture is set, firm to touch and golden brown.

Mushroom Stroganoff

Ingredients

3 tablespoons olive oil
1 tablespoon butter
500g fresh mushrooms (sliced)—button, oyster or shitakes
3 shallots (sliced)
2 garlic cloves (crushed)
300ml sour cream
1 tablespoon fresh parsley (chopped)

Method

Heat the oil and butter in a large frying pan and sauté mushrooms and garlic, stirring them until they are softened and just cooked. Add the shallots and cook for 1 minute. Season with salt and pepper to taste. Slowly stir in sour cream and heat mixture. Just before serving, stir in chopped parsley. Serve immediately.

Ratatouille

serves 6

Carbs 12g
per serve

Ingredients

2 medium eggplants

4 medium onions

4 large tomatoes

2 medium green capsicums

3 garlic cloves (crushed)

8 tablespoons olive oil

6 eggs

6 black olives (finely sliced)

Cracked black pepper and salt

Method

Cut unpeeled eggplants into 2cm rings and sprinkle with salt. Leave stand in dish for approximately 1 hour. Slice onions, capsicums and tomatoes into rings. In a medium saucepan arrange in layers, onions, crushed garlic, capsicums, drained eggplant with tomatoes on top. Sprinkle each layer with pepper and salt. Pour olive oil over vegetables. Cover and simmer slowly on top of stove for approximately 40 minutes. Transfer mixture to a casserole dish, mixing lightly to combine all ingredients. Make six slight depressions with back of a large spoon into top of mixture and break an egg into each one. Place casserole into a preheated moderate oven and bake for 15 minutes or until eggs are set. Sprinkle black olives over top before serving.

Soufflé Omelette

serves 1

Carbs 4g
per serve

Ingredients

2 eggs (separated)

2 tablespoons cold water

1 tablespoon fresh coriander (chopped)

½ tablespoon olive oil

2 teaspoon mango chutney

¼ cup cheddar cheese (grated)

Salt and pepper

Method

Beat egg yolks together with cold water, coriander, salt and pepper. Whisk egg whites until stiff peaks form and gently fold into egg yolk mixture. Heat the oil in a frying pan. Pour in egg mixture and reduce heat. Do not stir. Cook until the omelette becomes puffy and golden brown on the underside (carefully lifting one edge with a palate knife to check). Spoon on the chutney and sprinkle on the cheese. Fold over and slide on to a warm serving plate. Serve immediately.

SEAFOOD

Prawns with Avocado Mash

serves 4

Carbs 8g
per serve

Ingredients

1kg green tiger prawns
½ cup fresh basil leaves (chopped)
2 garlic cloves (crushed)
1 tablespoon lime rind (finely grated)
2 tablespoons peanut oil

Avocado Mash

2 medium avocados
2 tablespoons lime juice
2 medium tomatoes (seeded and chopped)
1 small red onion (chopped)
2 teaspoons ground cumin
2 tablespoons fresh basil leaves (chopped)

Method

Shell and devein prawns, leaving tails intact. Combine prawns in a large bowl with basil, garlic and lime rind. Cover and refrigerate for 3 hours or overnight. Heat oil in wok and stir fry prawns until they change colour.

Avocado Mash

Mash flesh of one avocado in a small bowl until smooth. Chop flesh of second avocado roughly then add to bowl of mashed avocado with remaining ingredients. Mix well. Spoon avocado mash onto serving dishes and divide equally onto each dish. Serve immediately.

Chilli Prawns with Shallots

Ingredients

1kg medium shelled green prawns

1 tablespoon hot chilli oil

½ cup minced shallots

1 small red chilli—minced

2 medium carrots—thinly sliced

2 medium stalks celery—thinly sliced

¼ cup chicken broth

½ cup chopped bok choy cabbage

½ cup fresh snow peas

2 tablespoons soy sauce

Method

Heat oil in a wok over high heat. Add garlic and prawns and cook till prawns change colour. Remove prawns and set aside—add shallots, red chilli, carrot and celery and stir fry for 30 seconds. Add the broth, cover and steam for 1 minute. Add bok choy, snow peas and soy sauce. Steam for 2 minutes until snow peas are tender but still crisp. Add prawns, heat through and serve.

Summer Salmon & Cottage Cheese Delight

Ingredients

1 envelope plain gelatine

¼ cup cold water

½ cup boiling water

¼ cup lemon/lime juice

1½ cups cottage cheese

1 large can salmon

½ cup sour cream

1 cup diced celery

1 cup chopped parsley

½ cup diced shallots

1 teaspoon salt and pepper

Method

Dissolve gelatine according to directions on packet. When dissolved, stir in salt and pepper, lemon juice and liquid from salmon. Allow to cool. Combine cheese with remaining ingredients excluding the salmon. Stir in gelatine mixture. Fold in salmon meat that has been mashed. Pour mixture into 9 x 5 x 3 inches (22 x 12 x 7 cm) loaf pan or suitable mould. Chill until firm. Serve with salad greens.

Garlic Prawns in Cream Sauce

serves 2

Carbs 6g
per serve

Ingredients

Green prawns (1kg)
3 tablespoons butter
3 cloves garlic, crushed
1 cup cream
Chopped shallots
Dash of dry white wine
Black pepper

Method

Melt butter and cook garlic until golden. Add green prawns and cook until just turned colour. Add the rest of the ingredients and bring to the boil quickly. Serve on a bed of steamed spinach or other suitable green vegetable.

Fish with Ginger Sauce

serves 1

Carbs 3g
per serve

Ingredients

White-fleshed fish, 1 serve, approximately 100g
1 teaspoon powdered ginger
1 teaspoon chopped parsley
1 teaspoon lemon/lime juice
Cracked black pepper to taste

Method

Butter or spray a sheet of foil big enough to wrap fish into a parcel. Place fillet on foil and fold. Before sealing foil pour prepared sauce over fish.

Sauce

Combine ginger, juice, parsley and pepper. Place sealed foil package onto baking tray and cook in preheated oven 100°C for approximately 10 minutes.

Salmon Surprise

Ingredients

1 large tin salmon (or tuna)
2 tablespoons chopped shallots
2 packets cream cheese
½ cup finely chopped parsley
½ teaspoon dry mustard

Method

Mash salmon. Combine cheese, mustard, shallots and blend thoroughly. Add salmon and mix well. Mould into balls and roll in parsley to coat.
Serve with green salad.

Prawns with Thai Salad

Ingredients

24 large green prawns
1 tablespoon oil
2 carrots (peeled)
100g bean sprouts
2 cups salad leaves
⅓ cup coriander leaves
⅓ cup mint leaves

Dressing

1 tablespoon lime juice
1 tablespoon fish sauce
1 tablespoon sugar substitute
2 teaspoons sesame oil

Method

Wash all salad leaves and herbs under running water. Tear leaves and herbs apart and place in a large bowl. Thinly slice carrot and toss through green salad. Add bean sprouts. Peel green prawns leaving the tails on. Cook prawns quickly (2-3minutes) in a fry pan or on a grill. The prawns will turn orange when cooked. Do not over cook. Add prawns to salad. Combine salad ingredients. Pour dressing over salad and serve immediately.

Prawns with Vegetables

Ingredients

60g snow peas
½ small carrot
60g baby corn
60g mushrooms
250g green prawns (peeled
with tail on)
1 small egg white (lightly beaten)
1 teaspoon cornflour
1 cup vegetable oil
1 shallot (cut into sections)
4 slices fresh ginger (peeled and
finely chopped)
½ teaspoon sugar substitute
1 tablespoon light soy sauce

Method

Top and tail the snow peas then cut in half. Slice carrot, mushrooms and baby corns, making sure all vegetables are about the same size. Place prawns in a bowl. Add egg white and cornflour paste and toss prawns until evenly coated. Preheat wok over high heat for 2-3 minutes and then add the vegetable oil. Add the prawns, stirring to separate them. Remove the prawns from the wok as soon as they change colour. Pour off the oil, leaving only 1 tablespoon in the wok. Add all the vegetables at once. Stir to combine. Add the prawns together with the ginger, sugar substitute and soy sauce. Toss all ingredients together. Transfer to a large serving dish. Serve immediately.

Helpful Hint
• When using wooden skewers for cooking kebabs, pre-soak in water. This prevents them burning during cooking.

Garlic Prawn Kebabs

Ingredients

16 large green prawns
8 teaspoons oil
⅓ cup dry white wine
4 large garlic cloves (crushed)

Method

Shell and devein the prawns. Leave tail and last segment of shell on. Mix oil, wine and garlic in a medium bowl and stir well. Place prawns in mixture and toss until well coated. Cover and marinate in refrigerator for at least 1 hour. If using bamboo skewers soak in water during this time to prevent burning during cooking. Thread prawns onto skewers, 4 on each skewer. Prawns can be cooked on a grill or in a fry pan. Brush prawns with marinade during cooking. Cook for 2-3 minutes, turning only once. Serve immediately on top of tossed green salad.

Prawn Fu Yong

Ingredients

2 tablespoons vegetable oil
1 medium carrot (grated)
5 eggs (beaten)
250g small raw prawns (peeled)

1 tablespoon light soy sauce
Pinch of Chinese five spice powder
2 shallots (chopped)
1 teaspoon sesame seeds

Method

Heat the vegetable oil in a preheated wok, swirling it around until oil is very hot. Add the grated carrot and stir fry for 1-2 minutes. Push the carrot to one side of the wok and add the beaten eggs. Cook, stirring gently for 1-2 minutes. Stir in prawns, light soy sauce and five spice powder into the mixture in the wok. Stir fry mixture for 2-3 minutes or until prawns change colour and mixture is almost dry. Turn mixture out onto a warm serving plate and sprinkle with chopped shallots and sesame seeds.

Scallops in White Wine

Ingredients

350g large scallops (rinsed)
¼ cup white wine
2 teaspoons olive oil
2 large handfuls of washed baby spinach
½ cup freshly grated parmesan cheese
Freshly ground black pepper

Method

Preheat oven to 180°C. Place scallops in a small baking dish, just large enough to hold scallops in one layer. Add the wine making sure each scallop is coated. Bake for approximately 12 minutes. Heat oil in a non-stick frying pan. Add the spinach and sauté for 2-3 minutes until wilted. Place spinach on a serving dish, add scallops and top with parmesan cheese.

Oysters Natural

Ingredients

2 dozen fresh oysters in shell
Rock salt
Lemon wedges

Method

Arrange 1 dozen of the oysters onto a serving dish which has had a layer of rock salt spread over the dish (the rock salt gives a base so the oysters will sit upright and make them easier to eat). Place lemon wedges on the side of the serving dish. Repeat for the second plate.

Oyster Shots

Ingredients

2 dozen oysters
¼ teaspoon Tabasco sauce
4 tablespoons pure cream
1 tablespoon lemon juice
½ tablespoon Worcestershire sauce

Method

Arrange oysters in four shot glasses. Combine all ingredients and spoon over oysters. Serve with lemon wedges.

Fish Fillets with Cream Sauce

Ingredients

800g white flesh fish fillets
1 large onion (sliced)
1 cup mushrooms (sliced)
2 tablespoons butter
¼ cup chopped parsley
1¼ cups dry white wine
Salt and pepper

Sauce

2 tablespoons butter
1 egg yolk
½ cup cream
¼ cup soy flour

Method

Melt butter in a shallow casserole dish. Arrange ½ sliced onion and ½ sliced mushrooms on bottom of the dish. Arrange fish fillets on top of vegetables and spread remaining onion and mushrooms on top of fish. Sprinkle parsley on top. Pour wine into dish. Cover casserole dish and place in preheated oven (180°C) for approximately 10-12 minutes—until fish is just cooked. Using a large spatula, remove fish and vegetables onto a large serving dish and keep warm.

Sauce Method

Melt butter in a saucepan, stir in flour and cook for 1 minute. Remove from heat, stir in reserved liquid from casserole dish and return to heat. Bring to boil, stirring continually then reduce heat and simmer until thickened. Combine beaten egg yolk and cream, stir into sauce mixture. Season with salt and pepper to taste. Place fish and vegetables onto serving plate and pour sauce over top. Serve immediately.

Trout in Butter Sauce with Almonds

Ingredients

4 cleaned trout
½ cup toasted almonds
1 teaspoon lemon juice
Soy flour
¾ cup butter
1 tablespoon parsley
Salt

Method

Sprinkle salt over trout. Lightly coat fish with flour. Preheat a fry pan. Melt ½ the butter in pan. Place fish gently in pan and cook till brown on both sides. Turning gently. Transfer fish to serving plate and keep warm. Add remaining butter to pan with lemon juice and toasted almonds. Simmer for a few minutes and pour over fish. Sprinkle with parsley. Serve with tossed salad.

Curried Fish

serves 4

Carbs 1g
per serve

Ingredients

1kg white fish fillets
Juice of 1 large lemon
1 teaspoon tumeric
2 teaspoons curry powder
Oil

Method

Wash and dry fish fillets and cut into required sized pieces. Sprinkle both sides with lemon juice, salt and pepper then place in dish with remaining lemon juice. Allow to stand 5 minutes then sprinkle with curry powder. Coat fish with mixture then remove and deep fry in hot oil for a few minutes until cooked.

Smoked Salmon Omelette

serves 4

Carbs 1.5g
per serve

Ingredients

6 eggs
⅔ cup cream
1 tablespoon warm water
⅔ cup sour cream
1 tablespoon lemon juice
220g smoked salmon
1 tablespoon parsley

Method

Whisk eggs lightly then whisk in cream. Pour ¼ of the mixture into heated, lightly oiled 22cm non-stick frying pan. Cook over medium heat, tilting pan until omelette is almost set. Run spatula around the edge of pan to loosen. Turn onto plate, cover to keep warm. Repeat making 4 omelettes. Combine the sour cream, water, parsley and juice in a small bowl. Fold omelettes into quarters, place on serving plate. Top each with equal amounts of salmon and dressing.

Salmon Fillets with Roasted Capsicum & Butter Sauce

Ingredients

1 small red capsicum
1 tablespoon olive oil
1 tablespoon salt
6 medium (1.2kg) salmon fillets (skin on)
125g butter (chopped)
1 garlic clove (crushed)
1 small fresh red chilli, seeded and chopped finely
1 teaspoon lemon juice
2 tablespoons chopped fresh
coriander leaves

Method

Roast capsicum under the grill or in a very hot oven until the skin blisters and blackens. Cover the capsicum in plastic for 5 minutes, then peel away the skin and chop the flesh finely. Rub oil and salt into the skin of the salmon, place salmon skin side up on an oiled oven tray. Grill under a preheated grill for approximately 8 minutes or until the skin is browned and crisp. Melt butter in a medium pan, add garlic and chilli, cooking and stirring until fragrant. Add capsicum, lemon juice and coriander, stirring until mixture is heated. Serve salmon with sauce.

Prawn Omelette

serves 4

Carbs 5g
per serve

Ingredients

6 eggs
2 tablespoons cream
1 tablespoon light soy sauce
1 tablespoon sesame oil

3 shallots (sliced finely)
1 small red capsicum (sliced finely)
250g small cooked, peeled prawns
1 tablespoon chopped fresh basil
15g butter

Method

Beat the eggs, cream and soy sauce together. Heat the sesame oil in a wok. Add the shallots and capsicum. Stir fry briskly for 2-3 minutes. Add the prawns and chopped basil to the wok and stir fry for 2 minutes. Transfer to plate and keep warm. Melt the butter in a large frying pan and add the beaten egg mixture. Cook over a medium heat until just set. Spoon the vegetable and prawn mixture in a line down the middle of the omelette, then fold each side of the omelette over. Transfer the omelette to a warmed serving dish and cut into 4 portions. Serve immediately.

Seafood Creole

serves 4

Carbs 8g
per serve

Ingredients

1 cup crabmeat (fresh or tinned)
200g cooked bay prawns
225 gm can tomatoes (diced)
3 medium onions (finely chopped)
1 large capsicum (finely diced)

3 celery sticks (finely diced)
¼ cup parsley (finely chopped)
3 tablespoons tomato paste
¼ cup water
Cracked black pepper and salt

Method

Pour tomatoes into a large pan. Add remaining ingredients except seafood. Bring ingredients to boil. Reduce heat and cover. Simmer gently for approximately 10-12 minutes. Stir through seafood. Reheat gently. Add extra cracked pepper to taste if needed. Serve immediately.

Salmon with Spicy Pesto

Ingredients

4 x 250g salmon steaks
2 tablespoons sunflower oil
1 lime (juiced)
pinch of salt

Pesto

4 fresh mild red chillies
2 garlic cloves
2 tablespoons sunflower seeds
1 lime (juiced)
5 tablespoons olive oil
Cracked black pepper

Method

Rub the sunflower oil into the salmon fillets. Place into a shallow dish. Pour lime juice over salmon and sprinkle with salt. Marinate in the fridge for approximately 2 hours.

Pesto

In a blender or food processor, place garlic cloves, sunflower seeds, seeded chillies and lime juice. Process until well mixed. Pour the olive oil gradually over the moving blades until the sauce has thickened and emulsified. Drain the salmon from its marinade. Grill the fish steaks for about 5 minutes on either side and serve with the spicy pesto.

Baked Fish with Cheesy Crust

serves 4

Carbs 5g
per serve

Ingredients

4 x 200g pieces cod or haddock skinned
1 tablespoon oil
2 tablespoons butter
1 onion (finely sliced)
1 garlic clove (chopped)
1 green capsicum (sliced)
400 gm tin chopped tomatoes and basil
2 tablespoons capers (chopped)
2 tablespoons almond meal
¼ cup cheddar cheese (grated)
2 teaspoon fresh parsley (chopped)
Salt and pepper

Method

Heat the oil and half the butter in a saucepan. Fry onion for approximately 4 minutes until softened. Add garlic, capsicum, chopped tomatoes and capers. Season with salt and pepper to taste. Cover and cook for 12-15 minutes, then uncover and simmer gently to slightly reduce liquid. Place the fish fillets in a buttered ovenproof dish, dot with the remaining butter and season with salt and pepper. Spoon the tomato sauce over the top. Bake in preheated 230°C oven for approximately 10-12 minutes. Mix together the almond meal, cheese and parsley in a bowl. Remove fish from oven and sprinkle cheese mixture over the top. Return to the oven and bake for a further 10 minutes. Remove fish from oven and let stand for 5 minutes. Carefully remove fish pieces to serving dish. Serve immediately.

Garlic Prawns in Pots

Ingredients

1 kg green king prawns
3 cups olive oil
125g butter
8 garlic cloves (crushed)
2 small red chillies (finely chopped)
1 tablespoon parsley (chopped)
Salt and pepper
Lemon wedges

Method

Shell prawns, leaving tails intact. With a small, sharp knife, make a slit down back of prawn, carefully remove back vein. Wash prawns under cold running water, then pat dry. Put ½ cup of oil into four individual heat proof pots or bowls. Add 30g butter into each dish. Mix together garlic and chillies. Divide mixture evenly between each of the four pots. Season with salt and pepper. Place dishes on an oven tray, and put in moderate oven for 10-15 minutes, until butter has melted and oil is very hot. Remove pots from oven and leave on tray. Divide prawns between the four dishes. Return to oven for approximately 10 minutes or until prawns are cooked. Cooking time will depend on size of prawns. Sprinkle with chopped parsley. Serve immediately.

Butter-Fried Salt & Pepper Prawns

serves 4

Carbs 6g
per serve

Ingredients

3 teaspoons sea salt

3 teaspoons cracked black pepper

¼ cup lemon pepper seasoning

3 tablespoons lemon rind (finely grated)

2 tablespoons dried onion flakes

1.5kg large green prawns (shelled and deveined with tails left on)

¼ cup peanut oil

4 shallots (sliced)

2 garlic cloves (crushed)

¼ cup fish stock

2 tablespoons sweet chilli sauce

Method

Combine salt and pepper, lemon seasoning, lime rind and onion flakes in a small bowl. Slice half way through each prawn from the back. Press prawns firmly into dry seasoning mixture, coating both sides. Place prawns on a tray and cover. Refrigerate for at least 1 hour. Heat 2 tablespoons of oil in a wok, stir fry prawns in batches until prawns have just changed colour. Put prawns aside and keep warm. Heat remaining oil in wok, stir fry shallots and garlic for 1 minute. Add prawns and fish stock and chilli sauce, stir fry tossing until mixture boils. Serve prawns with stir-fried green vegetables, if desired.

Calamari with Capers

Ingredients

800g calamari (cut into rings)
2 teaspoons lime rind (finely grated)
2 garlic cloves (crushed)
1 tablespoon fresh parsley (chopped)
1 tablespoon olive oil

60g butter (melted)
60ml lime juice
1 tablespoon Dijon mustard
1 tablespoon baby capers (drained)
240g curly endive

Method

In a large bowl, combine calamari, garlic and parsley. Stir to mix thoroughly, cover and refrigerate for 3 hours or overnight. Heat oil in a wok. Stir fry calamari in batches, until browned and tender. Do not over cook. Combine butter, lime juice, mustard and capers. Return all calamari to wok and pour over mixture. Stir fry, tossing until sauce boils. Serve calamari over a bed of curly endive.

Salmon with Herbed Sauce

Ingredients

4 salmon fillets (skinned and boned)
¼ cup cream
2 tablespoons fresh tarragon (chopped)
2 tablespoons butter

1 tablespoon oil
1 garlic clove (crushed)
½ cup dry white wine
½ cup parsley (finely chopped)

Method

Gently heat the cream in a small saucepan until just beginning to boil. Remove pan from the heat and stir in half the tarragon. Leave the herb cream to infuse. Heat the butter and oil in a frying pan and cook the salmon fillets for 3-4 minutes on each side. Remove from the pan and keep warm. Add the garlic to the pan and stir fry for 1 minute. Add the wine and let the mixture boil until it reduces to about 1 tablespoon. Strain the herb cream into the pan and cook for a few minutes, stirring continuously, until sauce has thickened. Stir in remaining tarragon and the parsley. Mix well. Spoon over salmon fillets. Serve immediately.

Ginger Fish

Ingredients

2 x 500g whole bream or snapper
(cleaned and scaled)
3 tablespoons soy sauce
6 shallots (cut into thin diagonal pieces)
2.5cm piece ginger (crushed)

water
3 tablespoons oil
5cm piece ginger extra (cut into
thin straws)
Salt

Method

Fill a shallow pan two thirds full with water. Add crushed ginger and salt. Bring liquid to the boil and boil for 5 minutes. Reduce heat, place whole fish in water, cover and cook for approximately 10 minutes or until cooked. Remove fish, drain well. Place fish on heated serving plates. Sprinkle ginger straws and shallot slices over each fish. Heat oil until very hot, add soy sauce, then pour over each fish. Serve immediately.

Scallops with Ginger Sauce

Ingredients

12 scallops, with coral left on
1 cup cream
3 teaspoons butter

3 shallots (diagonally sliced)
3cm piece fresh ginger
(peeled & finely diced)
Cracked black pepper and salt

Method

Melt butter in pan. Add the whole scallops and sauté for approximately 2 minutes until lightly browned. Do not over cook scallops as this will toughen them. Remove scallops with a slotted spoon and place on a plate and keep warm. Add ginger and shallots to the pan and stir fry for 2 minutes. Stir in cream and cook for 1-2 minutes until sauce has thickened. Season with cracked pepper and salt to taste. Place scallops on serving plates and pour sauce over. Serve immediately.

CHICKEN

CHICKEN

Tenderloin Spicy Chicken

serves 4

Carbs 0.5g
per serve

Ingredients

750g chicken tenderloin
1 teaspoon oil
1½ teaspoons five spice powder
2 cloves garlic (crushed)

Method

Combine chicken, oil, five spice powder and garlic in a bowl—let stand for ½ hour. Cook chicken in batches on heated oil grill plate or barbecue until browned and cooked through. Serve with salad or vegetables.

Indian Chicken

serves 6

Carbs 6g
per serve

Ingredients

1kg skinless chicken breasts, halved
1½ cups plain non-fat yoghurt
2 teaspoons cayenne pepper
2 teaspoons minced ginger
1 teaspoon ground coriander

2 garlic cloves, minced
2 teaspoons cumin
2 teaspoons mustard seeds
1 teaspoon paprika
¼ teaspoon allspice

Method

In a blender, combine all ingredients except chicken. Pour the marinade over the chicken breasts and marinate in the refrigerator for at least 2 hours or up to 48 hours. Grill the chicken for about 6 minutes per side until no trace of pink remains.

Spicy Chicken Breast

Ingredients

4 chicken breasts
4 teaspoons olive oil
1 teaspoon grated ginger
¼ teaspoon cayenne pepper
¼ teaspoon hot mustard
¼ teaspoon tumeric
3 teaspoons curry powder
2 teaspoons tomato sauce

Method

Mix oil, spices and sauce in a flat dish. Coat chicken in mixture, cover and marinate in fridge for 4 hours or overnight. Heat a heavy pan and cook, turning once, for approximately 8 minutes or until just cooked (do not overcook). Remove and slice. Serve with salad greens.

Summer Chicken Salad

Ingredients

500g boneless, skinless cooked chicken breast, cut into cubes
1½ cups sliced celery
½ cup diced red pepper (capsicum)
1 cup fresh snow peas, trimmed
1 cup diced, unpeeled red apples

Dressing

¼ cup vinegar
¼ cup canola oil
2 tablespoons sugar substitute
1 tablespoon celery seeds
Fresh ground black pepper and salt to taste

Method

Combine all salad ingredients. Whisk together the dressing ingredients. Pour the dressing over the salad and serve.

Lemon Chicken Stir-fry

Ingredients

3 whole boneless, skinless chicken
breasts cut into strips

2 tablespoons sesame oil

3 cups bean sprouts

2 garlic cloves, minced

2 teaspoons minced ginger

1 cup fresh snow peas, trimmed

½ cup sliced red capsicum

1 tablespoon lite soy sauce

1 tablespoon fresh lemon juice

1 x 170g can bamboo shoots

½ cup slivered almonds

Method

Heat 1 tablespoon of the oil in a wok over high heat. Add the bean sprouts and stir fry for 1-2 minutes until crisp. Remove from wok and place on a platter. In the remaining oil, stir fry the garlic and ginger for 30 seconds. Add the chicken and stir fry for approximately 4 minutes. Push the chicken up on the sides of the wok and add the snow peas and capsicum and stir fry for approximately 2 minutes. Combine the soy sauce and lemon juice. Add to wok along with the bamboo shoots. Move chicken back to the centre of the wok. Combine all ingredients and cook a further 2 minutes. Place chicken mixture over the cooked bean sprouts and top with almonds to serve.

Baked Chicken Breast

Ingredients

2 large chicken breasts cut in half
2 tablespoons cream
¼ teaspoon garlic salt
1 tablespoon butter
Salt and pepper to taste
2 teaspoons wheat germ
1 beaten egg

Method

Dry chicken breasts with paper towel. Sprinkle with salt and pepper and garlic salt. Beat egg and cream together. Dip each piece of chicken into egg mixture and then roll in wheat germ. Melt butter in a heavy based frying pan. Sauté chicken until golden brown and then place chicken into a baking pan and cover with foil. Place in preheated 180°C oven for approximately 20 minutes.

Crunchy Chicken Salad

Ingredients

½ tablespoon olive oil
1 chicken breast (skinless)
2 tablespoons mayonnaise (egg-based)
1 teaspoon Dijon mustard

Juice of 1 lemon or lime
2 celery stalks
½ cup bean sprouts
¼ cup chopped shallots

Method

Place oil in a pan and cook chicken over medium heat until thoroughly cooked (6-7 minutes per side). In a small bowl combine mayonnaise, mustard and lemon/lime juice. Drain chicken and cut into strips and mix with dressing in the bowl. Add chopped celery, sprouts and shallots.

Chicken with Mustard Marinade

Ingredients

3 boneless, skinless chicken breasts, halved

3 garlic cloves, minced

6 shallots finely chopped

½ cup lite soy sauce

2 tablespoons Dijon mustard

1 tablespoon oyster sauce

1 tablespoon hoisin sauce

1 cup low-fat low-sodium chicken broth

2 teaspoons sesame oil

2 teaspoons honey

Method

In a blender, combine all ingredients except chicken. Pour the marinade over the chicken breasts and marinate in the refrigerator for at least 2 hours or up to 48 hours. Grill chicken both sides. Cook until no trace of pink remains.

Grilled Chicken & Avocado

Ingredients

1 large chicken breast
½ cup avocado (mashed)
½ cup cheese (grated)
Juice of 1 lemon
2 teaspoons butter

Method

Slice chicken breast in half to make 2 flat pieces. Place chicken in shallow dish and marinate in lemon juice for approximately 10 minutes. Melt butter in frying pan. Add chicken and pour lemon juice over the top. When chicken is just cooked, drain on paper towel. Spread mashed avocado over chicken and sprinkle grated cheese on top. Place under grill till cheese is melted.

Chicken & Macadamia Nut Salad

Ingredients

2 large chicken breasts (cooked)
2 large gherkins (chopped)
3 hard boiled eggs (chopped)
3 shallots (washed, chopped & trimmed)

½ teaspoon freshly ground black pepper
½ cup sugar free mayonnaise
¼ cup sour cream
3 tablespoons fresh dill (chopped)
½ cup macadamia nuts

Method

Cut chicken breast meat into strips. Mix all other ingredients. Add chicken and toss.

Stuffed Chicken Breast with Mustard Sauce

serves 4

Carbs 1g
per serve

Ingredients

4 chicken breast fillets
3 tablespoons butter
2 tablespoons oil

Filling

3 tablespoons butter
3 shallots (thinly sliced)
1 garlic clove (crushed)
170g canned crabmeat

2 teaspoons lemon juice
1 tablespoon cream
Cracked black pepper to taste

Sauce

3 tablespoons butter
¾ cup water
¼ cup dry white wine
3 tablespoons seeded mustard
1 tablespoon cream

Method

Melt butter in pan. Add sliced shallots and crushed garlic. Cook for 1 minute. Add drained crabmeat, lemon juice, cream and black pepper. Cook for further minute.

Cut a pocket in chicken fillet, thickest side, without cutting right through. Fill pockets with prepared filling. Heat oil and butter in pan, add fillets and cook until golden on both sides. Remove and place on greased ovenproof dish. Cover and bake in moderate oven for approximately 20 minutes.

Sauce

Melt butter in pan. Add water, wine, mustard and cream.

Chicken Kebabs

Ingredients

Chicken breast (cut into 2cm cubes)

1 onion (quartered)

1 red capsicum (cut into cubes)

1 zucchini (cut into cubes)

Soy sauce

¼ cup oil

Method

Thread chicken and vegetables onto skewers (skewer can be pre-soaked in water to prevent burning). Grill or barbecue basting with sauce and oil. Turn frequently to coat with sauce.

Light Chicken Rolls

Helpful Hint
• Always remove all seeds and membrane from capsicums before cooking as they are very bitter.

Ingredients

1 cup chicken (cooked and diced)

½ cup red capsicum (diced)

½ cup cucumber (diced)

2 hard-boiled eggs (sliced)

1 shallot (diced)

Black pepper to taste

Lettuce leaves

½ cup mayonnaise (see page 141)

Method

Combine all ingredients in a large bowl. Chill at least 20 minutes. Place heaped tablespoons in lettuce leaves and roll up.

Chicken Patties

Ingredients

500g chicken mince
1 onion (finely chopped)
2 cloves garlic (minced)
1 zucchini (grated)
1 small red capsicum (finely chopped)

1 tablespoon paprika
1 tablespoon soy sauce
1 egg (lightly beaten)
1 tablespoon fresh parsley (chopped)
Olive oil

Method

Combine ingredients thoroughly. Form the mixture into 12 patties. Pour oil into heated pan. Place patties on pan and turn after 3-4 minutes. Repeat. Serve with tossed salad.

Chicken Supreme

Ingredients

2kg chicken pieces
125g bacon (diced)
100g butter
1 cup red wine
1 cup chicken stock

3 cloves garlic
1 bay leaf
1 large onion (diced)
3 cups mushrooms (sliced)
Salt and pepper to taste

Method

Sauté diced bacon in butter until golden. Remove from pan and save. Wash and dry chicken pieces thoroughly, then brown in pan. Remove and set aside. Sauté onions and mushrooms. Return chicken and bacon to pan. Add chicken stock, garlic, wine and bay leaf. Simmer gently 40-50 minutes in uncovered skillet. Add salt and pepper to taste. Remove bay leaf prior to serving.

Chicken with Ginger & Lime

Ingredients

250g chicken breast meat

125 ml olive oil

2 teaspoons sesame oil

2 tablespoons lime juice

Grated rind and juice of 1 orange

1 tablespoon grated ginger

1 garlic clove (crushed)

2 teaspoons light soy sauce

3 shallots (finely chopped)

1 teaspoon sugar substitute

250g assorted salad leaves

Method

Cook chicken breast in fry pan with 1 tablespoon olive oil. Lightly brown both sides then reduce heat and cook for a further 3 minutes. Remove from pan and allow to cool. Slice chicken meat into thin slices.

Dressing

Blend olive oil and sesame oil with the lime, orange rind and juice, grated ginger, garlic, soy sauce, shallots and sugar until well blended.

To Serve

Arrange assorted salad leaves on a serving dish. Top with chicken slices and drizzle with salad dressing.

Chicken Florentine

Ingredients

2 skinless chicken breasts
(cut in halves)
6 teaspoons soy flour
3 tablespoons basil (shredded)
1 garlic clove (crushed)
¼ cup grated parmesan cheese
½ teaspoon salt
¼ teaspoon pepper
1 teaspoon oil
500g fresh spinach or
1 packet, 250g, frozen spinach

Method

Place flour, salt and pepper on a flat dish and mix well. Coat each chicken piece (one at a time) with flour mixture. Tap off excess mixture and place chicken to one side. In a frying pan heat oil to medium heat. Add chicken pieces and gently cook, turning once. Cook approximately 10 minutes or until cooked through. Meanwhile, wash and drain fresh spinach. Place spinach, basil and garlic in a large saucepan with ¼ cup water and cook until spinach is wilted (approximately 2 minutes). Drain off any excess liquid. Toss mixture with a fork. Place spinach on a serving plate and arrange hot chicken on top. Sprinkle with parmesan cheese and serve immediately.

Chicken Marengo

Ingredients

1½kg chicken breast meat

2 cup mushrooms (sliced)

½ cup shallots (chopped)

3 medium sized tomatoes (chopped)

1 cup chicken stock

1½ cups dry white wine

2 tablespoons soy flour

2 cloves garlic (crushed)

2 tablespoons oil

Salt and pepper to taste

Method

Dice chicken into bite sized pieces. Heat oil in a large frying pan, add garlic and chicken pieces. Only cook enough chicken in pan so that chicken can cook and be moved around to enable it to brown on all sides (do 2 batches if necessary). Remove cooked chicken from pan and put to one side. Add flour to juices in pan and cook for 1 minute. Add wine and stock gradually, stirring until mixture boils and thickens. Season with salt and pepper. Add mushrooms, shallots and tomatoes. Cook approximately 5 minutes. Return chicken to pan, cover and simmer for approximately 30 minutes.

Crumbed Chicken

Ingredients

4 chicken breasts (cut into 8 pieces)
1 cup almond meal
1 cup parmesan cheese
2 tablespoons parsley (finely chopped)
2 eggs beaten
4 tablespoons butter (melted)
Pepper and salt

Garlic Mayonnaise

½ cup whole egg mayonnaise
½ cup cream
2 garlic cloves (crushed)

Method

Mix together almond meal, parmesan cheese, parsley, salt and pepper in a shallow dish. Dip the chicken pieces in the beaten egg, then into the crumb mixture. Place on a baking sheet on a tray and chill in the refrigerator for at least 30 minutes.

Preheat oven to 180°C. Drizzle or lightly brush melted butter over the chicken pieces and cook in oven for approximately 20-25 minutes, until crisp, golden and cooked through.

Mayonnaise

Mix egg mayonnaise, cream, garlic, salt and pepper to taste. Spoon mayonnaise into a small serving bowl and serve with chicken pieces. Great with a crisp green salad.

Chicken Casserole

Ingredients

1½ kg chicken pieces (skinless)
225g butter
1 garlic clove (crushed)
½ cup dry white wine

150ml cream
1 tablespoon parsley (chopped)
Paprika
Pepper and salt

Method

Melt butter in a large pan. Add garlic and stir fry for 1 minute. Add chicken pieces and brown on all sides. Remove chicken and place into a greased casserole dish. Set aside and keep warm. Add wine, pepper and salt to pan and bring to the boil, stirring continuously. Pour liquid over chicken pieces, cover casserole and bake in moderate oven for approximately 45 minutes or until chicken is tender. Stir cream into casserole juices and blend well. Return chicken to oven for 5 minutes. Before serving, sprinkle top with parsley and paprika.

Helpful Hint
• If using wooden skewers, pre-soak in cold water to prevent them catching fire under grill.

Tandoori Chicken Kebabs

Ingredients

4 chicken breasts (diced into pieces)
1 tablespoon lemon juice
3 tablespoons tandoori paste
3 tablespoons sour cream
1 garlic clove (crushed)

2 tablespoons fresh coriander (chopped)
1 small onion, (cut into wedges and in layers)
Salt and pepper
Oil for basting

Method

Place chicken in a bowl and add lemon juice, tandoori paste, cream, garlic, coriander, salt and pepper. Mix well and cover chicken pieces. Cover and leave in fridge to marinate for 2-3 hours. Preheat grill. Thread alternative pieces of marinated chicken and onion onto four or six skewers. Brush lightly with oil, lie on a grill rack and cook under a high heat for 10-12 minutes, turning only once.

Lemon Chicken

Ingredients

4 whole chicken breasts (can be halved)
4 tablespoons butter
1 medium onion (finely diced)
1 tablespoon parsley (finely chopped)

1 lemon (juiced)
1 tablespoon lemon rind (grated)
Cracked black pepper and salt
Lemon slices to garnish

Method

Preheat grill on moderate. In a small saucepan, melt butter, then add onion, parsley and lemon juice and rind. Season with salt and pepper. Heat mixture through, do not boil. Remove from heat. Brush the chicken breasts generously with the herb mixture. Place under grill and cook for 10-12 minutes, basting frequently with the herb mixture. Turn chicken over and baste again, then cook for a further 10-12 minutes, or until chicken is cooked. Continue to baste frequently. Serve chicken garnished with lemon slices and any remaining herb mixture.

Chicken with Red Cabbage

Ingredients

8 chicken thighs
1 onion (chopped)
8 cups red cabbage (finely shredded)

4 tablespoons butter
½ cup red wine
¾ cup walnuts (shelled)
Ground black pepper and salt

Method

Heat butter in pan and lightly brown chicken pieces. Transfer to a plate. Add the onion to the pan and sauté gently until soft and light brown. Stir the cabbage through the onion, season with salt and pepper. Cook over a moderate heat for 6-7 minutes, stirring once or twice. Stir through the walnuts. Transfer chicken pieces to a large casserole dish. Place cabbage mixture on top. Pour over red wine. Cover casserole dish and cook in preheated moderate oven for approximately 40-50 minutes until chicken is well cooked and cabbage tender.

Sweet Chilli Chicken with Almonds

Ingredients

700g chicken breasts (sliced thinly)

¼ cup fresh coriander (finely chopped)

2 chillies (seeded and finely chopped)

1 tablespoon sesame oil

1 garlic clove (crushed)

2 tablespoons peanut oil

¼ cup sweet chilli sauce

2 tablespoons lime juice

¾ cup raw almonds (toasted)

1 cup snow peas (sliced thinly)

Method

Marinate chicken with coriander, chilli, sesame oil and garlic in a large bowl. Cover and refrigerate for at least 3 hours. Heat peanut oil in wok, stir fry chicken mixture in batches until browned and cooked through. Return all chicken to wok and add chilli sauce and lime juice and stir fry until sauce boils. Add almonds and snow peas, stir fry until mixture is all heated through.
Serve immediately.

Chicken & Capsicum Casserole

Ingredients

1½ kg chicken breasts (skinless)
3 large capsicums (red, green and yellow)
2 large onions (finely diced)
2 garlic cloves (finely chopped)
½ cup dry white wine
1 x 400g can diced tomatoes
6 tablespoons olive oil

Method

Wash the capsicums. Prepare by cutting them in half, scooping out the seeds. Slice into strips. Heat half the oil in a large saucepan and cook the onion over gentle heat until soft. Remove onion to a side dish.

Add remaining oil to pan. Add the chicken pieces and brown them on all sides, cook for approximately 6-8 minutes. Return the onions to the pan, and add the garlic. Pour in the wine and cook until liquid has been reduced by half.

Add the capsicums and stir until all mixture is well coated. Season to taste. Stir in tomatoes. Lower the heat, cover the pan and cook for approximately 25-30 minutes. Casserole will be cooked when chicken is cooked and capsicums are soft.

Stir thoroughly before placing on serving dish.

BEEF

Beef Burger with Blue Cheese Dressing

serves 4

Carbs 1g
per serve

Ingredients

500g lean beef mince

3 tablespoons chopped parsley

2 egg yolks

2 teaspoons mustard

4 teaspoons mayonnaise (egg-based)

100g blue cheese—finely crumbled

Salt and pepper to taste

Method

Blend together mince, parsley, egg yolks, salt and ground black pepper. Shape mixture into burger sized patties. Spray non-stick pan with oil.
Cook burgers until browned and cooked through. Serve with green salad and dressing.

Dressing

Mix together mustard and mayonnaise then fold through cheese.

Carpet Bag Steak

serves 4

Carbs 0g
per serve

Ingredients

1 piece rump steak—approx 1kg

1½ dozen oysters

Salt and pepper to taste

Butter

Method

Make pocket in steak, rub pocket with salt and pepper. Stuff oysters into the pocket and secure with skewers. Grill or pan fry in butter to desired degree. Cut into serving pieces.

Beef Stroganoff

Ingredients

1kg rump or fillet steak
1 teaspoon salt
250g sliced mushrooms
Pepper
1 medium onion (diced)
1 tablespoon butter
½ cup sour cream

Method

Cut meat into thin strips. Melt butter in pan and fry onion, add meat and cook until almost done. Add sliced mushrooms and continue frying until meat is tender. Pour in sour cream, season to taste and heat through gently.

Beef in Red Wine

Ingredients

1kg beef mince
Dash of Tabasco sauce
6 tablespoons dry red wine
Salt and pepper to taste
1 teaspoon paprika

Method

Combine all ingredients and blend thoroughly. Place in greased loaf pan and bake in preheated hot oven for approximately 1 hour.

Hamburger Steaks

serves 5

Carbs 1.8g
per serve

Ingredients

1kg beef mince
1 cup beef bouillon
1 egg (beaten)
Salt and pepper to taste
1 teaspoon dry mustard
¼ teaspoon garlic powder
2 tablespoons Worcestershire sauce

Method

Combine all ingredients except bouillon. Slowly add bouillon and then shape into hamburger patties. May be pan-fried or grilled.

Grilled Fillet Steak

serves 4

Carbs 0g
per serve

Ingredients

4 fillet mignon steaks
2 teaspoons olive oil
Salt (lite) to taste
5 tablespoons coarsely cracked black peppercorns

Method

Rub each steak with some of the oil. Place peppercorns on a plate and press steaks into the peppercorns to coat. On a medium grill place the fillets, turning once according to how well done you desire the meat. A good guide is 10 minutes for rare; 15 minutes for medium and 18 minutes for well done.

Beef Goulash

Ingredients

1kg round steak (diced)

1 tablespoon fat or butter

Salt and freshly ground black pepper

1 medium onion (diced)

2 bay leaves

3 teaspoons sugar substitute

1 tablespoon flour

1 tablespoon paprika

Pinch allspice

¼ cup cold water

Pinch thyme

¼ teaspoon vinegar

Method

In pan melt fat and brown beef. Season with salt and pepper. Add onion, bay leaves and thyme. Pour sweetener over all. Cover and simmer for approximately 1½ hours. Combine flour, paprika, allspice, water and vinegar and stir in. Cook for approximately 10 minutes or until sauce is thickened. Remove bay leaves and serve.

Tasty Beef Stew

Ingredients

1kg chuck steak diced

1 tablespoon fat or butter

1½ teaspoons lite salt

¼ teaspoon pepper

1 sprig parsley

¼ teaspoon thyme

2 bay leaves

1 teaspoon Worcestershire sauce

1 large onion sliced

1 stalk celery diced

3 sliced carrots

Method

Brown meat in melted butter in casserole dish.

Add seasonings and Worcestershire sauce. Cover casserole and simmer until meat is tender. Add uncooked vegetables to meat about ½ an hour before meat would be tender.

BBQ Steak

Ingredients

1kg sirloin steak
1 teaspoon chilli powder
2 teaspoons minced ginger
2 cloves garlic minced
1 small onion finely minced
⅓ cup lemon juice
2 tablespoons olive oil
2 teaspoons paprika

Method

Combine all marinade ingredients. Add the steak and marinate in fridge overnight. On a medium heat barbecue place the steak and turn once, cooking until desired tenderness. 30 minutes approximately for medium and 40-45 minutes for well done. Carve into thin slices and serve.

Steak Dianne

Ingredients

1kg fillet steak
¾ cup butter
2 tablespoons Worcestershire sauce

Freshly ground pepper
1 clove crushed garlic
1 tablespoon brandy
2 tablespoons chopped parsley

Method

Pound steak until quite thin. Season each side with pepper. Put butter into pan and add steak once butter is sizzling. Add garlic to steak—turn steak and add Worcestershire sauce and brandy to pan. Swirl steak in pan juices. Cook to your liking and add chopped parsley.

Helpful Hint
• Marinate
meat prior to
freezing. The
meat will
marinate
further while
defrosting.

Steak Kebabs

Ingredients

1kg rump steak

1 red capsicum

1 green capsicum

4 medium mushrooms

2 medium onions

Marinade

1 tablespoon oil

3 tablespoons red wine

1 tablespoon lemon juice

1 tablespoon soy sauce

1 clove crushed garlic

Pinch mustard

Pinch ground thyme

Method

Cut meat into cubes. Combine marinade ingredients and add steak—stir until well mixed. Cover and refrigerate overnight. Peel onions in halves. Wash capsicum, remove seeds and cut into squares. Remove stalks and peel mushrooms.

Thread vegetables and meat on skewers as follows: first onion, then meat, green pepper, meat, red pepper, meat and lastly top with mushroom cap.

Cook under grill turning frequently and brushing with any remaining marinade.

Asian Beef Stir-fry

Ingredients

500g lean beef strips
1 tablespoon soy sauce
2 tablespoons dry white wine
2 tablespoons oyster sauce
2 cloves crushed garlic
½ cup chopped shallots

1 cup cauliflower florets
1 cup sliced mushrooms
½ cup red capsicum sliced
½ cup green capsicum sliced
1 cup snow peas
¾ cup beef stock

Method

Lightly spray wok or non-stick deep pan with oil.
Add beef strips and sauté until browned. Remove from pan. Add all vegetables
to wok and stir fry until cooked. Stir in wine, soy sauce, oyster sauce and beef
stock. Return beef to mixture and lightly stir through.

Beef & Vegetable Lasagne

Ingredients

2 tablespoons oil

1 onion (diced)

500g mince

1 capsicum (diced)

2 tablespoons tomato paste

1 stock cube (beef) & 2 cups water

2 eggs (slightly beaten)

½ cabbage

½ bunch spinach

8 zucchini (sliced)

1 cup tomato juice (unsweetened)

Parmesan cheese

Method

Heat oil, brown onion and mince. Add rest of ingredients for sauce and simmer for 15 minutes. Allow to cool slightly. Mix in eggs. While simmering meat, prepare vegetables. Cut woody section (core) from cabbage. Pour boiling water over and let stand 10 minutes. Separate leaves gently. Remove stalks from spinach. Using a square casserole dish, place one layer of cabbage over base then proceed with a thin layer of mince, layer of zucchini, layer of capsicum, layer of spinach, layer of mince. Finish with rest of cabbage. Pour over tomato juice. Sprinkle with parmesan cheese. Bake in 150°C oven for 30-40 minutes or until cooked.

Asian Beef Parcels

Ingredients

Vermicelli

350g lean beef mince

½ cup bean sprouts

2 stalks lemon grass (finely chopped)

1 tablespoon lemon juice

1 tablespoon soy sauce

2 spring onions (thinly sliced)

200g can water chestnuts (drained)

12 rice paper wrappers

12 fresh mint leaves

Method

Place vermicelli into a bowl, cover with boiling water and allow to stand for 10 minutes or until soft. Drain well. Place the beef mince and 3 tablespoons of water into a frying pan. Cook over a high heat for about 10 minutes or until the beef is tender and cooked. Drain off any excess liquid. Transfer the beef to a bowl, add the bean sprouts, lemon grass, lemon juice, soy sauce, spring onions and water chestnuts. Soak one rice paper wrapper at a time in a bowl of water. Take out of water and place on a clean cloth. Put a tablespoon of mixture in centre of each wrapper. Place a mint leaf at the end of each wrapper, fold in the ends and roll up to enclose.

Beef Rolls

Ingredients

Rump or topside beef thinly sliced
(as much as desired)
12 spinach leaves (stalks removed)
2-4 tablespoons sour cream
½ onion (diced)
1 cup mushrooms (sliced)

Chopped parsley
1 egg (slightly beaten)
Black pepper
2 tablespoons oil
2 cubes beef stock
½ cup cream

Method

Beat meat until thin. Layout beef slices and place one spinach leaf on top of each one. Combine sour cream, onion, mushrooms, parsley, lightly beaten eggs and black pepper. Using a teaspoon, form balls from mixture and place on top of spinach leaf. Roll up gently to form a parcel. Tie with string or secure with skewers. Heat oil, brown each roll quickly and place them in a casserole dish. Pour over stock, cover and bake for 1 hour or until tender. Cream may be added to the juice (in casserole) before serving, boil for 2 minutes and use as a sauce.

Pepper Beef and Asparagus

Ingredients

700g eye fillet in 4 pieces
6 Roma tomatoes

2 bunches fresh asparagus
Freshly crushed pepper
Salt

Method

Season the beef with cracked pepper and salt. Using a very hot frying pan, seal beef on both sides. Place meat in oven dish and cook in oven at 150°Celsius for 20-25 minutes. Blanch asparagus by plunging into boiling water for approximately 2 minutes and then rinsing under cold water to stop the cooking process. Cut Roma tomatoes in half and oven roast until brown on top. Bring meat from the oven and let stand for 5 minutes before slicing thinly. Arrange tomatoes, meat and asparagus on serving dish and serve immediately.

Italian Beef Burgers

Ingredients

400g lean mince
1 small onion
½ cup English spinach (chopped)
¼ cup tomato (chopped)
¼ cup feta cheese (crumbled)
4 Kalamata olives (pitted and finely chopped)
2 tablespoons parsley (chopped)
1 teaspoon tomato paste
Salt and pepper to taste

Method

Combine all ingredients in a large bowl. Mould 2 beef patties. Grill or pan fry over medium high heat for approximately 5 minutes each side. Serve immediately.

Basic Meatloaf

serves 6

Carbs 4g
per serve

Ingredients

1½kg minced meat (lamb, beef, pork or veal)
2 tablespoons chilli powder
1 tablespoon paprika
3 eggs
3 cloves garlic
3 tablespoons parsley
250g cheddar cheese (grated)
2 tablespoons Worcestershire sauce
Salt to taste

Method

Preheat oven to 180°C. In a large bowl, mix all ingredients. Place meat mixture into oiled loaf pan and bake for 45 minutes to 1 hour.

Savoury Mince

serves 4

Carbs 4g
per serve

Ingredients

2 tablespoons oil
1 onion (diced)
1kg mince (beef, veal, lamb)
½ cup capsicum (finely diced)
½ cup mushrooms (sliced)
2 tablespoons tomato paste
Crumbed beef stock cube
½ cup water
Dash Worcestershire sauce
½ cup cheese (grated)
Black pepper and salt substitute
Chopped parsley

Method

Heat oil in pan, add onions and mince, brown well. Add rest of ingredients, stirring well, cook 15-20 minutes or until meat is tender. Sprinkle with parsley before serving.

Spicy Beef Balls

serves 4

Carbs 6g
per serve

Ingredients

1kg beef mince

1 egg

1 onion (finely chopped)

4 tablespoons parsley (finely chopped)

4 tablespoons fresh basil (finely chopped)

Salt and pepper

Method

Combine mince, onion, egg, herbs and spice in a bowl. Knead well. Cover and chill for approximately 1 hour (chilling helps the mixture hold together. Form mixture into meatballs, about the size of golf balls. Place meat into a preheated, oiled frying pan. Do not overcrowd pan. Allow enough room so the meatballs can be moved around to ensure even cooking. Cook approximately 10 minutes.

Mexican Chilli

serves 4

Carbs 6g
per serve

Ingredients

¼ cup onion (diced)

¼ cup red capsicum (diced)

¼ cup mushrooms (chopped)

500g ground beef

1 x 250 gram can (small) tomatoes

2 teaspoons chilli powder

1 teaspoon Tabasco sauce

Salt and pepper to taste

Method

Spray pan with non-stick cooking spray. Sauté onion and capsicum then add mushrooms and stir though. Set aside. Brown beef and drain off any fat. Combine in a deep saucepan or casserole dish, the beef and vegetable mixture together with tomatoes and enough water to achieve desired thickness. Blend in chilli powder, salt and pepper and Tabasco sauce. Simmer for approximately 30 minutes. Add extra seasoning if desired.

Veal Steaks with Creamy Garlic Sauce

Ingredients

2 tablespoons butter
1 clove garlic (crushed)
4 veal steaks
1 onion (diced)
2 cups mushrooms (sliced)

½ cup chicken stock
½ cup cream
1 teaspoon mustard (French)
Black pepper and salt
Fresh parsley (chopped)

Method

Melt butter, add garlic and cook steaks gently, turning once, till tender and golden. Remove to a plate. Add onions and mushrooms to pan and cook 4 minutes. Pour in stock, cream, mustard, salt and pepper, stirring, bring to the boil for 2 minutes. Return veal to pan and allow to heat through only. Serve veal with sauce poured over and sprinkle with fresh parsley.

Spicy Veal Steak

serves 4

Carbs 0.5g
per serve

Ingredients

4 veal T-bone steaks
1 teaspoon ground coriander
1 teaspoon ground cumin
2 teaspoons grated lemon rind
½ teaspoon ground garlic cloves
1 tablespoon olive oil

Method

Combine veal, spices, rind and olive oil in bowl. Refrigerate for 4 hours or overnight. Cook on heated oiled grill plate or barbecue until browned and cooked as desired. Serve with salad or vegetables.

Sesame Veal Schnitzel

serves 6

Carbs 1g
per serve

Ingredients

6 veal cutlets
2 eggs (beaten)
½ cup parmesan cheese (grated)
4 tablespoons olive oil
3 tablespoons sesame seeds
¼ teaspoon oregano
¼ teaspoon garlic powder

Method

To make schnitzel coating, mix cheese, sesame seeds, garlic powder and oregano into a shallow dish. Dip cutlets into seed mixture, then into beaten egg, then back into mixture, making sure veal is coated. Heat oil in pan. Cook veal for a few minutes on each side until lightly browned.

Beef in Burgundy

Ingredients

1½ kg round steak (cut into large cubes)

30g butter

2 tablespoons oil

12 small onions (peeled)

60g bacon rashes (cut into large pieces)

250g button mushrooms (sliced)

60g butter extra

1 garlic clove (crushed)

2 tablespoons gluten flour

2 cups dry red wine

3 beef stock cubes

3 cups water

Salt and pepper

Method

Heat butter and oil in a pan. Add a quarter of the steak at a time to pan and brown well on all sides, remove from pan and repeat the process with all remaining meat. Add onions to pan and cook until golden brown. Add bacon, cook until crisp, then add sliced mushrooms, cook for approximately 1 minute. Remove from pan. Heat butter in pan, add garlic, cook for 1 minute. Add flour, cook until dark golden brown, do not allow to burn. Remove pan from heat, gradually add water and wine, stir until well combined. Return to heat, add crumbled stock cubes, salt and pepper, stir until sauce boils and thickens. Put meat and bacon in ovenproof dish, pour sauce over, mix. Cook covered in moderate oven for 1 hour, remove from heat, add onions and mushrooms, stir until combined. Return to oven, cook covered a further 30 minutes or until meat is tender.

Spicy Beef & Vegetables

serves 4

Carbs 10g
per serve

Ingredients

700g beef steak (sliced thinly)

¼ teaspoon five spice powder

1 tablespoon black bean sauce

1/3 cup oyster sauce

1 tablespoon peanut oil

1 medium onion (sliced)

2 medium carrots (sliced)

500 gm can bamboo shoot slices (drained and chopped)

150g snow peas (sliced)

Method

Combine beef, five spice powder, black bean sauce, oyster sauce and garlic into a bowl, cover and refrigerate for 3 hours. Heat oil in wok, stir fry beef in batches, then onion until browned. Remove from wok and keep warm. Stir fry carrot until just tender. Return beef and onion to wok and mix with carrot. Add bamboo shoots and snow peas. Toss until well combined.
Serve immediately.

Savoury Meatloaf

serves 4

Carbs 3g
per serve

Ingredients

1 kg minced beef

1 garlic clove (minced)

2 tablespoons parsley (chopped)

1 tablespoon curry powder

1 tablespoon soy sauce

2 eggs (beaten)

100g tasty hard cheese (grated)

Salt and pepper

Method

Add all ingredients together in a large mixing bowl. When mixture has been well combined, put into a greased loaf pan. Press mixture down well into pan. Place in a pre-heated 200°c oven and cook for approximately 40 minutes.

Beef & Capsicum Stir Fry

Ingredients

400g steak (sliced into strips)

2 tablespoons soy sauce

2 tablespoons sesame oil

1 tablespoon barbecue sauce

1 garlic clove (finely chopped)

1 tablespoon ginger root (grated)

1 red capsicum (sliced)

1 yellow capsicum (sliced)

1 cup snow peas (topped and tailed)

4 shallots (cut into pieces)

2 tablespoons oyster sauce

Method

In a bowl, marinate beef strips with soy sauce and barbecue sauce. Cover and leave for approximately 30 minutes. Heat oil in a wok. Stir fry garlic and ginger quickly, about 30 seconds. Add the capsicums, snow peas and spring onions and stir fry over a high heat for 3 minutes. Add the beef and any juices left from marinade into the wok and stir fry for a further 3-4 minutes. Pour the oyster sauce and add ¼ cup water if needed. Stir until well combined. Serve immediately.

Beef Khorma

Ingredients

800g minced beef
1½ tablespoons butter
2 medium onions (sliced)
2 garlic cloves (crushed)
1 large red chilli (finely chopped)
3 teaspoons fennel seeds

1½ teaspoon cumin seeds
1 teaspoon ground turmeric
1 teaspoon ground cardamom
1 cup beef stock
2 small tomatoes (chopped)
⅓ cup fresh parsley (chopped)

Method

Heat butter in a large pan, cook onion stirring until brown. Add garlic, chilli and spices. Cook, stirring continuously until fragrant. Add minced beef. Cook mixture until beef is browned and well cooked. Add stock and bring mixture to the boil. Cover and simmer for approximately 20 minutes. Remove lid and continue to cook until liquid has evaporated, stirring occasionally. Just before serving, add chopped tomatoes and parsley to add colour. Serve immediately.

Devilled Kidneys

Ingredients

8 lamb kidneys
½ cup butter
1 medium onion (chopped)

1 garlic clove (crushed)
½ cup fresh parsley (finely chopped)
1 tablespoon Worcestershire sauce
Salt and pepper

Method

Soak kidneys in lightly salted water for approximately 20 minutes. Rinse kidneys, remove skin and any fat and cut in half. Heat butter in a fry pan, add onion and garlic, sauté until soft but now browned. Add kidneys, cook gently on both sides. Add salt and pepper, Worcestershire sauce and parsley. Stir until mixture is well combined. Serve immediately.

Home-style Pot Roast

Ingredients

2kg piece of topside

3 large carrots

8 small onions

3 medium parsnips

5 cups beef stock

2 tablespoons tomato paste

1 teaspoon Worcestershire sauce

1 teaspoon mixed herbs

⅓ cup soy flour

90g butter

Method

Peel carrots, onions and parsnips. Cut carrots and parsnips into large pieces. Leave onions whole if small. If large, cut in half. Leave vegetables aside. In a large pan, heat 30g of butter. Add the piece of topside. Brown well on all sides. Remove meat from pan, cover with foil and set aside.

Add vegetables to pan and sauté with meat juices until all are golden brown. Remove vegetables from pan. Melt remaining butter in pan, add flour, stir over high heat until flour is brown. Remove pan from heat, add stock and stir until well combined. Add sauces, herbs, salt and pepper. Return pan to heat, stirring until sauce boils and thickens. Place meat into a large pot, pour sauce over top and bring to boil. Reduce heat, cover and simmer gently for approximately 2 hours. Add vegetables and simmer for a further 30 minutes or until all vegetables are tender. Place meat and vegetables on a serving platter. Bring sauce in pan to boil and simmer until a gravy consistency. Pour over meat and vegetables. Serve immediately.

Steak in Red Wine

serves 4

Carbs 2g
per serve

Ingredients

4 fillet steaks
2 cups red wine
2 tablespoons butter
4 shallots (finely chopped)
½ cup cream
Salt and pepper

Method

Heat one tablespoon of butter in pan, add steaks, cook until browned. Remove steaks from pan and keep warm. In same pan, melt one tablespoon of butter and shallots and cook for 1 minute. Add wine, cook quickly until liquid has been reduced to half original quantity. Slowly stir in cream. Season with salt and pepper. Continue stirring until sauce boils. Boil for 1 minute. Return steaks to pan to reheat. Pour sauce over steaks. Serve with salad or vegetables.

PORK

Thai Pork Balls

Ingredients

500g pork mince

2 tablespoons fresh ginger (finely chopped)

2 tablespoons fresh coriander (chopped)

1 tablespoon soy sauce

1 egg (lightly beaten)

2 garlic cloves (finely chopped)

½ teaspoon sesame oil

1 teaspoon fish sauce

1 teaspoon sweet chilli sauce

1 tablespoon oil (cooking)

Method

In a large bowl, place all ingredients except oil for cooking. Mix well to combine. Form into small balls or patties. Place on a baking tray, cover and refrigerate for 1 hour. Heat oil in a large frying pan. Cook pork balls in batches, for 5-6 minutes or until brown and cooked through. Serve with steamed green vegetables.

Ham & Bacon Quiche

Ingredients

1 large onion diced

½ cup cream

1 cup zucchini grated

1 cup bacon bits

5 eggs beaten

½ cup diced ham

¼ cup grated cheese

Method

Combine all ingredients and pour into greased baking dish. Bake at 180°C for 45 minutes or until set.

Apricot Ham Steak

Ingredients

6 ham steaks
2 teaspoons Dijon mustard
¼ cup sugar free apricot jam
2 teaspoons cider vinegar

Method

In a bowl mix together jam, mustard and vinegar. Grill ham steaks, brushing with the basting sauce and turning once, basting the other side. Cooking time approximately 8 minutes.

Teriyaki Pork

Ingredients

6 pork loin chops
1 sachet sugar substitute
¼ cup soy sauce
3 cloves minced garlic
¼ cup dry sherry
1 tablespoon peanut oil

Method

Combine all marinade ingredients. Add the pork chops and marinate in fridge for 12 hours. Grill the chops or barbecue until tender.

Western Asian Pork

Ingredients

1kg pork tenderloin, cut into strips
1 tablespoon dry sherry
2 teaspoons cornstarch
1 teaspoon cumin
2 cloves garlic, minced

Salt and pepper to taste
1 tablespoon canola oil
1 green pepper—seeded and cut into strips
1 medium onion, thinly sliced
12 cherry tomatoes, cut into halves

Method

Combine sherry, cornstarch, cumin, garlic, salt and pepper in a container with a lid. Add pork and shake to coat. Heat oil in pan over medium-high heat. Add pork mixture and stir fry for a few minutes. Add remaining ingredients and steam covered for 4-5 minutes.

Summer Ham Rolls

Ingredients

75g Philadelphia cream cheese

2 tablespoons hot water

8 thin slices of ham

1 tablespoon chopped chives

3 chicken stock cubes

Method

Separate and place slices of ham onto a plate.

Dissolve chicken stock cubes in hot water and mix with cream cheese. Spread mixture over ham slices. Sprinkle chives over top with salt and pepper. Roll ham slices and secure with toothpicks.

Tasty Egg & Bacon Salad

Ingredients

6 hard-boiled eggs

¼ cup mayonnaise (egg-based)

6 cooked bacon rashers

Salt and pepper to taste

1 medium tomato

Lettuce leaves (approximately 8)

¼ teaspoon dry mustard

Method

Wash and pull apart lettuce leaves and place in serving bowl. Chop eggs and bacon and quartered tomato together. Fold together mayonnaise and mustard, salt and pepper. Add egg mixture to lettuce and drizzle dressing over salad and serve.

Pork Satay Sticks

makes
approx. 12

**Carbs 1g
per serve**

Ingredients

250g pork fillets, cut into
5mm pieces
2 teaspoons soy sauce
1 teaspoon tomato sauce

½ teaspoon chilli powder
1 teaspoon cumin
2 tablespoons oil
¼ teaspoon curry powder
Extra oil

Helpful Hint
• Pre soak
bamboo
skewers to
prevent them
burning during
cooking.

Method

Place meat in a bowl, add remaining ingredients and mix well. Cover and
refrigerate at least 3 hours or overnight. Thread meat onto bamboo skewers.
Preheat a grill plate and brush with oil, add skewers and cook quickly. Brush
with extra oil during cooking if needed.

Sauce

¾ cup crunchy peanut paste
½ teaspoon sweet chilli sauce
¼ to ½ cup water

Method

Combine ingredients, adding enough water for pouring consistency, and heat
slightly in microwave. Serve with satay sticks.

Pork Loin & Celery Casserole

Ingredients

1 tablespoon oil
4 tablespoons butter
1 kg loined, rolled loin of pork with rind removed
1 onion (chopped)
150ml dry white wine

150ml water
6 celery sticks, cut into 2.5 cm lengths
150ml cream
1 tablespoon lemon juice
Salt and ground black pepper

Method

Heat oil and half the butter in a heavy casserole dish, just large enough to hold the pork and celery, then brown the pork evenly. Transfer the pork to a plate. Add the onion to the casserole and cook until softened but not browned. Place the pork on top and add any juices.

Pour the wine and water over the pork, season to taste, cover and simmer gently for 30 minutes. Turn the pork, arrange the celery around it, cover again and cook for approximately 40 minutes, until the pork and celery are tender. Transfer the pork and celery to a serving plate, cover and keep warm. Stir the cream into the casserole, bring to the boil and add lemon juice. Slice the pork, pour some sauce over slices. Serve the remaining sauce separately.

Asian Pork

Ingredients

800g pork fillets (sliced thinly)
2 garlic cloves (crushed)
500g green beans (halved)

2 tablespoons peanut oil
1 medium onion (chopped)
1 tablespoon lemon juice
80g butter

Method

In a saucepan of boiling water, cook beans until just tender. Remove immediately from boiling water and place in cold water to stop cooking process and so they retain a fresh green colour. Drain and set aside.

Heat oil in wok, stir fry pork and onion together in batches until browned. Return all pork and onion mixture to wok, add beans, butter, lemon juice and garlic. Stir fry, tossing until well combined.

Serve immediately.

Hot & Spicy Ribs

Ingredients

1.5 kg pork spare ribs (chopped)
2 tablespoons peanut oil
2 garlic cloves (crushed)
2 teaspoons fresh ginger (grated)

2 tablespoons tomato sauce
2 tablespoons sweet chilli sauce
1 tablespoon fresh coriander (chopped)

Method

Place spare ribs in a large pan of boiling water. Cook uncovered for approximately 10 minutes or until just tender. Drain spare ribs. Heat oil in wok, stir fry spare ribs in batches until well browned and cooked through. Return all spare ribs to wok and add all remaining ingredients, stir fry tossing continuously until sauce boils and all ribs are well coated.

SAUCES, DIPS & STOCKS

Garlic Butter Sauce

Ingredients

½ cup melted butter

2 cloves garlic (crushed)

Pinch salt

1 teaspoon chives (mixed)

Method

Combine all ingredients in a saucepan and cook for 1-2 minutes.

Dianne Sauce

Ingredients

Use leftover pan juices

2 cloves garlic (crushed)

½ teaspoon Worcestershire sauce

2 tablespoons tomato paste

1 cup cream

Splash brandy

Method

Combine all ingredients and boil for 4-5 minutes.

Bernaise Sauce

Ingredients

½ cup melted butter
2 tablespoons lemon juice
3 egg yolks
1 bay leaf
1 teaspoon chopped parsley
2 tablespoons dry white wine

2 teaspoons dried tarragon
1 tablespoon tarragon vinegar
2 teaspoons shallots (finely chopped)
2 teaspoons sugar substitute
½ teaspoon prepared mustard
Salt and pepper to taste

Method

Blend together butter, lemon juice, egg yolks, parsley, mustard, salt and pepper. Gently simmer wine, tarragon, bay leaf, vinegar, shallots and sugar substitute in a saucepan until quantity is reduced by approximately half. Remove bay leaf. Combine other ingredients in blender until smooth. Combine all ingredients and reheat lightly.

Gravy for Roasts

Ingredients

Pan juices from roast
1 tablespoon tomato paste
Dash lemon juice
1 cup cream
1 teaspoon soy sauce
½ teaspoon Vegemite
1 teaspoon parsley (chopped)

Method

After draining off all excess fat, combine all ingredients with pan juices and heat gently, stirring constantly until mixture boils.

Hollandaise Sauce

serves 4-6

Carbs 1g
per serve

Ingredients

3 egg yolks
3 teaspoons dry mustard
1 teaspoon wine vinegar
¼ teaspoon salt
Pinch cayenne pepper
2 tablespoons cream
6 tablespoons butter

Method

Combine all ingredients except butter. Heat gently until mixture thickens. Stir in butter slowly until sauce is creamy.

Seafood Sauce

makes 3 cups

Carbs 12g
per serve

Ingredients

½ cup tomato paste
1 green capsicum minced
½ teaspoon shallots (chopped)
¼ teaspoon chives (chopped)
2 cups mayonnaise (sugar free)

Method

Cook tomato paste over low heat, stirring constantly until thickened. Allow to cool and combine with remaining ingredients. Chill and serve with seafood.

Guacamole Dip

Ingredients

1 ripe tomato

2 limes

1-2 large avocados

½ onion (finely chopped)

¼ teaspoon ground cumin

¼ teaspoon mild chilli powder

1 tablespoon fresh coriander
(finely chopped)

Method

Place tomato in a bowl and cover with boiling water and leave it to stand for 30 minutes. Drain and plunge the tomato into cold water and the skin will slide off easily. Cut in half, deseed and chop the flesh. Squeeze the juice from the limes into a small bowl. Cut avocado in half and peel skin off carefully. Dice the flesh and toss in the bowl of lime juice to prevent flesh discolouring. Mash coarsely. Add the chopped onion, tomato, cumin, chilli powder and fresh coriander to avocado. Transfer to a serving dish. Serve with celery fingers or bacon rind crackers.

Mustard Cream Sauce

Ingredients

300ml thickened cream
¼ cup dry white wine
1 tablespoon mild English mustard

Method

Combine all ingredients in a pan, bring to the boil. Simmer until sauce thickens, stirring constantly.

Mayonnaise

Ingredients

2 eggs
1-2 tablespoons lemon juice
½ teaspoon mustard powder
½ teaspoon sugar substitute
250ml oil
Salt and pepper
Dash Tabasco, Worcestershire or soy sauce

Method

Combine all ingredients in blender.
Blend until smooth. Keep refrigerated.

makes approx 1.5 cups

Carbs 10g per serve

Great for chicken, steak and veal.

makes 250ml 1 cup

Carbs 2g per serve

Helpful Hints
• Thin mayonnaise if it's too thick by adding 1 tablespoon of hot water.
• Refrigerate homemade mayonnaise in a covered, non-reactive container and use within one week.

Lime Butter

Ingredients

250g butter (softened)
2 teaspoons grated lime rind
1½ teaspoon lemon juice
1 teaspoon chopped fresh dill
½ teaspoon grated fresh ginger

Method

Beat butter in a bowl with electric mixer until pale. Stir in remaining ingredients. Spoon mixture onto foil, wrap firmly and shape into a rectangle. Refrigerate until firm.

Homemade Chicken Stock

Ingredients

1 whole chicken carcass
2 stalks of celery
1 medium onion
1 bay leaf
¼ teaspoon basil
¼ teaspoon oregano
6 whole peppercorns
4 litres water

Method

Break up carcass and add giblets or extra chicken (raw or cooked). Combine all ingredients in a large saucepan. Bring to boil and simmer on low heat for 2 hours. Remove bay leaf. Cool and strain. Freeze for future use.

Zucchini & Garlic Dip

serves 4

Carbs 4g
per serve

Ingredients

1 cup cottage cheese

2½ cups steamed zucchini (chopped)

2 bacon rashers (fried, cooled and chopped)

3 teaspoons slivered almonds

¼ teaspoon parsley (chopped)

Salt and pepper to taste

¼ teaspoon shallots (chopped)

1 garlic clove (crushed)

Method

Place zucchini in saucepan with enough water to cover. Cook until just tender. Remove from heat and cool. In a blender, combine zucchini, cottage cheese, herbs and spices. Blend until smooth and fold in chopped bacon pieces and almonds. Place mixture in serving bowl and surround with celery fingers or pork rind chips.

DESSERTS, CAKES & BISCUITS

Peaches & Strawberries with Champagne

serves 6

Carbs 11g per serve

Ingredients

- 1 cup plain non-fat yoghurt
- 3 tablespoons champagne
- 2 teaspoons vanilla
- 1 sachet sugar substitute
- 1½ cups sliced peaches
- 1½ cups strawberries

Method

Combine champagne, yoghurt, vanilla and sugar substitute. Mix well. Place a layer of fruit into individual serving bowls or fluted glasses. Spoon on champagne yoghurt. Repeat layering yoghurt and fruit, ending with yoghurt. Garnish each dessert with half a strawberry.

Sparkling Jelly & Yoghurt

serves 4

Carbs 6.25g per serve

Ingredients

- 1 packet low-cal jelly crystals (any flavour)
- 500ml low fat yoghurt
- 250ml diet lemonade

Method

Add 250ml boiling water to 1 sachet jelly crystals. Stir until fully dissolved. Add 250ml cold low-cal (diet) lemonade. Allow to cool to room temperature. Using an electric mixer beat in yoghurt till smooth. Pour into individual serving bowls or glasses, top with strawberry and chill until set.

Custard Cream

Ingredients

3 cups milk

5 eggs

2½ teaspoons liquid sugar substitute

Dash salt

1 teaspoon vanilla essence

Nutmeg or cinnamon

Method

Heat milk (do not boil). Beat eggs together with salt, vanilla and sweetener. Stir in hot milk. When well mixed, pour into individual moulds and sprinkle with nutmeg or cinnamon. Place moulds into a baking or similar dish and fill with hot water ½ way up sides of the moulds. Bake in slow 150°C oven for approximately 40-45 minutes. Custard is ready when a blade is inserted around edge and comes away clean.

Strawberry Delight

Ingredients

1 cup cottage cheese

½ teaspoon salt

1 cup heavy cream, whipped

1 cup fresh hulled strawberries

½ teaspoon vanilla essence

Sweetener to taste

1 egg white

Method

Beat cottage cheese until smooth. Fold in whipped cream and vanilla. Beat egg white with salt until stiff. Strawberries, hulled and washed, are mashed with sweetener. Combine cheese and cream mixture with egg white mixture. To serve, fill small dishes or tall glasses alternately with cream mixture then strawberries. Chill.

Pavlova

Ingredients

6 egg whites
pinch of cream of tartar
1½ teaspoons of vinegar
1½ml liquid sweetener

¼ teaspoon vanilla
2 small bananas
3 medium passionfruit
2 cups heavy cream

Method

Beat egg whites with cream of tartar and a pinch of salt until soft peaks form. Fold in vanilla, vinegar and sugar substitute and beat until stiff.

Spoon mixture into greased pavlova tin. Bake in slow oven for approx 1-1½ hours. Remove and allow to cool. Decorate with whipped cream, sliced bananas and passionfruit.

Chocolate Mousse

Ingredients

2 x 75g blocks lite chocolate
1 tablespoon brandy
4 eggs, separated
1 cup cream

Method

Chop chocolate roughly and put in a double saucepan, stir over hot water until melted. Remove from heat and add egg yolks and brandy. Gradually beat until mixture is smooth and thick. Whip cream. Do not over-whip or the cream will be difficult to fold in—cream should be nicely thickened. Fold into chocolate mixture. Beat egg whites until soft peaks form. Here again do not over beat the whites or they will not easily fold into the chocolate mixture. Fold half the egg whites into the chocolate mixture then fold in the remaining half. It's much easier to do in two portions than if you add them all at once. Spoon mixture into 4 individual dishes or one large dish. To serve top with cream and grated chocolate. This popular dessert can be made a day ahead.

Coffee Cream Desserts

Ingredients

1 cup cream
Sweetener equal to ⅓ cup sugar
2 tablespoons instant coffee
½ teaspoon vanilla essence
2 teaspoons cocoa

Method

Combine all ingredients and refrigerate 1-2 hours. Whip until mixture is stiff. Place into individual serving dishes. Makes 2 cups.

Cheesecake Cups

serves 6

Carbs 1g
per serve

Ingredients

- 1 packet plain gelatine
- 1 cup boiling water
- 500g cream cheese
- ¾ cup sugar substitute
- 1 teaspoon vanilla essence

Method

Place patty liners in a muffin tin. Cut cream cheese into small cubes. Put boiling water into mixing bowl and sprinkle gelatine on top, stir until dissolved. Put cream cheese cubes into dissolved gelatine along with sugar substitute and vanilla essence. Beat well with an electric mixer. Pour mixture into patty liners. Refrigerate 2-3 hours until firm. Decorate with cream if desired.

Rainbow Jelly Treat

serves 8

Carbs 3g
per serve

Ingredients

- 1 packet sugar free strawberry jelly
- 1 packet sugar free lime jelly
- 1 packet sugar free orange jelly
- 3 packets sugar free lemon jelly
- 1 cup whipping cream

Method

Prepare first 3 flavours of jelly crystals separately, using 1½ cups of water each. Refrigerate each in shallow pans until set. Cut each flavour into small cubes. Mix all 3 packets of lemon jelly with 2¾ cups water. Allow to thicken. When mixture is nearly set, very thick but not firm, add cream, thicken again, and fold in all cut jelly cubes. Place mixture into suitable mould and chill until firm.

Mini Cheesecakes

Ingredients

1 packet digestive biscuits (finely crushed)
1 large egg
4 tablespoons sugar substitute
250g cream cheese (softened)
1 tablespoon fresh lemon juice
1 tablespoon grated lemon zest

Requires

12 cup mini muffin tin
12 fluted paper cups

Method

Preheat oven to 180°C. Place the paper cups in the muffin tin and distribute the crushed digestive biscuit among the cups. Put all ingredients into a food processor and blend thoroughly. If no food processor available; beat eggs, sugar and lemon juice together well with a whisk, then blend in softened cheese. Fold in lemon zest. Spoon mixture into cups. Bake for approximately 15 minutes or until the edges are set and the centre is still moist. Remove the cheesecakes from the muffin tin and let cool. Refrigerate for at least 1 hour before serving.

*Mini
esecakes*

Icy Pops

Icy Pops

Ingredients

375ml (1½ cups) diet soft drink

6 tablespoons cream

Method

Mix all ingredients together. Pour into plastic ice block moulds and allow to freeze overnight.

Vanilla Ice-cream Supreme

Ingredients

5 egg yolks

3 teaspoons vanilla extract

½ teaspoon cinnamon

2 tablespoons sugar substitute

¼ cup water

2 cups heavy cream (whipped)

Method

Place egg yolks, vanilla extract, sugar substitute and water in a blender. Blend at medium speed for 30 seconds. Fold egg yolk mixture into whipped cream. Blend well, being careful not to break down volume of whipped cream. Pour into refrigerator tray. Freeze for 2 hours.

Sponge Cake

serves 8

Carbs 3g
per serve

Ingredients

6 eggs (separated)
2 tablespoons sugar substitute
1 teaspoon vanilla essence

1 teaspoon grated lemon rind
3 tablespoons soy flour
4 tablespoons heavy cream
½ teaspoon cream of tartar

Method

Preheat oven to 160°C. Cover bottom of cake tin with baking paper, grease sides with butter or oil. Place egg yolks and sugar substitute in a bowl. Beat until well blended. Add vanilla essence and lemon rind, continue to beat and add soy flour 1 teaspoon at a time, beat until well blended. Add heavy cream. Beat egg white and cream of tartar until stiff. Fold yolk mixture into whites, being careful not to break down egg whites. Turn into tin and bake at 160° for 30 minutes.

Tropical Almond Cake

Ingredients

2 naval oranges*
4 thin-skinned limes*
Cooking spray
3 eggs
4 egg whites
1½ cups sugar substitute
1 teaspoon baking powder
225g almond meal
Whipped cream to serve

Method

Preheat oven to 190°C. Lightly spray a 22cm springform tin with cooking spray and line with baking paper. Scrub oranges and limes. Place oranges in a large saucepan of boiling water and simmer for 1 hour. Add limes and continue cooking for 1 hour or until fruit is very soft. Remove fruit from water and allow to cool. Cut fruit in half and remove seeds. Place fruit, including skins into a blender or food processor and blend until smooth. Using an electric mixer or hand blender, beat eggs, egg whites, sugar and baking powder until thick and pale. Fold in almond meal and pureed fruit mixture. Spoon mixture into tin. Bake for approximately 1 hour, or until skewer inserted into centre comes away clean. Place cake tin on wire rack and allow to cool. Serve with whipped cream if desired.

*Note: Fruit pieces should weigh approximately 375g each.

Baked Almond Flan

Ingredients

5 eggs
1 cup heavy cream
5 teaspoons sugar substitute
½ cup crushed almond flakes
1 cup water
2 teaspoons almond extract

Method

Preheat oven to 160°C.

Whip all ingredients, except almond flakes, for 3-4 minutes. Pour into large baking dish or 4 individual dishes. Sprinkle top with crushed almond flakes. Place dish in large container ½ full of water. Bake for approximately 40 minutes or until set.

Deluxe Mud Cakes

Ingredients

250g chocolate, sugar free or lite bars

3 eggs

2 tablespoons brandy

¾ cup ground almond meal

½ cup cream (whipped)

Requires

12 cup muffin tin

Method

Preheat oven to 150°C. Grease muffin tin and line bases with baking powder. Put chocolate in a heatproof bowl. Half fill a saucepan with water and bring to the boil. Remove from the heat and stir the bowl over the pan, making sure it is not touching the water. Stir occasionally until chocolate has melted. Place eggs and brandy in a bowl. Put the bowl over a saucepan of simmering water on a low heat, making sure the bowl does not touch the water. Beat the mixture with electric beaters on high speed for approximately 3½ minutes or until light and foamy. Remove from heat. Using a metal spoon, quickly and lightly fold melted chocolate and almond meal into the egg mixture until just combined. Fold in cream and spoon into muffin tin. Place pan in shallow roasting tin. Pour enough hot water into tin to come half way up sides of muffin tin. Bake for approximately 40 minutes or until just set. Remove muffin pan from water and cool to room temperature. Cover with plastic wrap and refrigerate overnight. Remove cakes from muffin tin and serve with cream.

Savoury Cheese Biscuits

Ingredients

150g butter, cut into small pieces
150g soy flour
150g mature cheese (grated)
1 egg yolk
Sesame seeds for sprinkling

Method

Grease baking tray with a little butter. Mix the flour and cheese together in a mixing bowl. Add butter to mixture with your fingertips. Stir in egg yolk and mix to form a dough. Wrap the dough in glad wrap and chill in refrigerator for about 30 minutes. On a lightly floured surface, roll out and cut 6cm rounds with cookie cutter. Place the round on the baking tray and sprinkle with sesame seeds. Bake in a preheated oven, 200°C. Cook until lightly golden.

Macadamia Nut Cookies

Ingredients

1 cup ground macadamia nuts
4 tablespoons sugar substitute
2 teaspoons vanilla
2 eggs (separated)
1 cup butter
1 large tablespoon soy flour
¼ cup macadamia nuts (chopped)

Method

Preheat oven to 160°C. Cream egg yolks with sugar substitute. Beat egg whites until stiff and set aside. Cream together all ingredients except the chopped macadamia nuts and fold in egg whites. Place mixture, 1 tablespoon at a time, on a buttered cookie sheet. Place macadamia nuts on top and bake for about 40 minutes or until golden brown.

makes 35

Carbs 2g
per serve

Helpful Hint
• Allow biscuits to stand on baking trays for 5 minutes before transferring to a wire rack. This gives them time to firm and prevents them from breaking.

makes 12

Carbs 2g
per serve

Chocolate Brûlees

Ingredients

600ml pure cream

240g lite chocolate (finely chopped)

6 egg yolks

½ cup sugar substitute

Method

Preheat oven to 150°C. Place cream and chocolate in a medium heavy based saucepan and stir over medium heat for 10 minutes or until chocolate melts and mixture is combined. Remove from heat. Using a whisk, combine the egg yolks and ⅓ cup of sugar substitute until pale and creamy. Gradually stir in the cream mixture until combined. Place six, 125ml capacity ramekins in a baking tray. Pour chocolate mixture evenly into ramekins. Pour enough boiling water into baking dish to reach halfway up the sides of ramekins. Bake on lowest shelf of preheated oven for approximately 50 minutes or until brûlees are firm around the edges. Remove baking dish from oven. Remove ramekins from water and set aside for 1 hour to cool. Cover with plastic wrap and refrigerate for 8 hours or overnight to set. Preheat grill on high. Sprinkle brûlees with remaining sugar. Cook under grill about 6cm from heat source, for 1 minute or until sugar bubbles and caramelises. Allow to cool slightly before serving.

Almond Cream Custard

serves 2

Carbs 4g
per serve

Ingredients

100ml cream
25ml full cream milk
¼ teaspoon almond essence
1 egg
1 tablespoon flaked almonds
2 teaspoons sugar substitute

Method

Preheat oven to 180°C. Combine cream, milk, sugar, almond essence and egg in a small bowl. Divide mixture between two oven-proof ramekins. Sprinkle almonds on top. Bake for approximately 30 minutes or until custard is set.

Baked Berry Delights

serves 4

Carbs 3g
per serve

Ingredients

300g thawed frozen mixed berries
(eg raspberries & strawberries)
1 cup pure cream

1 teaspoon vanilla essence
4 egg yolks
¼ cup sugar substitute

Method

Preheat oven to 180°C. Combine the thawed berries in a bowl. Divide the mixture between four ramekins. Combine cream and vanilla and bring to the boil over medium heat. Remove from heat. Whisk together the egg yolks and sugar substitute in a heatproof dish. Whisk in the hot cream mixture. Strain through a fine sieve into a clean saucepan. Stir over low heat for 5 minutes or until custard simmers and thickens slightly. Pour the custard among prepared dishes. Pour enough boiling water into a roasting pan to reach halfway up the sides of the dishes. Bake in preheated oven for 30 minutes, or until just set. Remove pan from oven. Remove ramekins from water and serve immediately.

Chocolate Meringues

Ingredients

1¼ cups sugar substitute

2 tablespoons cocoa powder

4 egg whites

¼ teaspoon cream of tartar

Method

Preheat oven to 110°C. Sift sugar and cocoa powder together. In a large bowl, beat egg whites and cream of tartar with electric beaters on medium speed until peaks form. Beat in sugar one tablespoon at a time. Beat on high speed until mixture is glossy and stiff. Line baking trays with baking paper. Drop rounded teaspoons of mixture onto sheets, leaving space between meringues. Bake at 110°c for 40-45 minutes or until tops of meringues feel dry to the touch. Cool for 5 minutes on trays then remove.

VITAMINS & MINERALS

Vitamin A

Promotes healthy eyes, skin, hair and also maintains the mucous membranes of the lungs and intestines. Improves immunity.

Beta Carotene

(Can be converted by the body to Vitamin A).One of the carotenoids—antioxidants that provide the yellow and orange colours in fresh produce. It improves immunity and protects against the effects of ageing and some cancers.

Vitamin B Group

Provides energy. Important and natural function of the nervous system. Needed for healthy skin, hair, nails and eyes.

Vitamin C

Provides collagen, which is needed for healthy skin, bones, cartilage and teeth. Provides stress response and helps the body to absorb iron.

Vitamin D

Needed to absorb calcium and phosphorous for healthy bones and teeth.

Vitamin E

Antioxidant. Needed for healthy circulation and healthy muscles including the heart. Heals scar tissue.

Calcium

Maintains healthy bones and teeth. Regulates nerve and muscle function. Also needed for blood clotting.

Iron

Carries oxygen to the body cells via the blood.

Potassium

Maintains nerves, cells and muscle and promotes normal blood pressure and heartbeat.

CARBOHYDRATE COUNTS

Alcohol: BEER

	Carbohydrate grams per serve GMS CH
Standard or Midstrength Beer, average 200ml glass	6
Standard or Midstrength Beer, 375ml can/bottle	11
Light Beers: Export Light, 375ml	7
2.2 Lite (Tooheys), 375ml	8.5
Carlton Light Special Light, 375ml	10
XXXX DL (Castlemaine), 375	3
Hahn Premium Light, 345ml	12
Tooheys Blue, 375ml	17
Stout, average, 375ml	14
Guinness (Carlton), 375ml	18
Cider, 375ml, sweet	25
Cider, 375ml, dry, Strongbow	11

ALCOHOLIC SODAS, PREMIXES ETC

Bacardi Breezers, Watermelon, 275ml	17
Bacardi Breezers, other varieties, 275ml	24
Metz, Ice Storm, 275ml	29
Smirnoff Baltik, 300ml	39
Stoli Ruski, all flavours, 300ml	33

SubZero Alcoholic Soda, 330ml	19
UDL Cans, 375ml, Vodka with Melon	26
UDL Cans, 375ml, other varieties	39

WINE, SPIRITS, LIQUEURS

Red/Claret, 120ml	0
Rose, 120ml	2
White: Dry/Chardonnay, 120ml	0.3
Medium/Sauterne, 120ml	1.3
Champagne, 120ml	1.2
Port/Muscatel, average, 60ml	7
Sherry, sweet, 60ml	6
Sherry, dry, 60ml	1
Brandy & Dry, Gin, Tonic, 120ml	11
Vermouth, dry, 60ml	2
Vermouth, sweet, 60ml	9
Baileys Irish Cream, 30ml	5.5
Bacardi, Bourbon, Rum and Cola, 120ml	12
Brandy, Rum, Gin, Whiskey	0
Liqueurs, average, 30ml	13

BISCUITS (Per Biscuit)

SAVOURY	GMS CH
Shapes (average), Counter	1.5
Jatz, Savoy, Breton	2.5
Salada	9.5
Thin Captain, Vita Weat, Cruskits	4

SWEET	
Granita, Nice	8.5
Milk Arrowroot	6.5
Tim Tam, Choc Royals	12

BREAD, BUNS etc

White bread, 1 slice, 25g	12
White bread, 1 slice, 30g	14
White bread, toasting, 1 slice, 35g	16
Brown bread, 1 slice, 30g	13
Wholemeal bread, 1 slice, 30g	13
Multigrain/Granary/Kibble bread, 1 slice, 30g	14
Rye bread, light, 1 slice, 30g	14
Rye bread, dark, 1 slice, 30g	14
Fruit loaf, light, 1 slice, 30g	15
Fruit loaf, heavy, 1 slice, 30g	16

	GMS CH
Lebanese/Pocket/Flatbread/Pita bread, white, 50g	25
Lebanese/Pocket/Flatbread/Pita bread, wholemeal, 50g	24
Bagels, plain, medium, 55g	37
Bagels, Sara Lee, average, 85g	50
Bread rolls, dinner, small, 30g	14
Bread rolls, French roll, medium 45g	20
Bread rolls, sandwich roll/bun, 65g	26
Bread rolls, wholemeal roll/bun, 65g	25
Crispbreads, average, white, each	5
Crispbreads, average, rye/whole wheat, each	5
Croissants, plain, 50g	20
Croissants, Sara Lee All Butter, each	19
Croissants, filled with ham and cheese, 125g	30
Crumpets, average, 50g	20
Crumpet Breaks, Tip Top, 71g	25
Fruit or Hot Cross Buns, 55g	27
Matzo, 17cm/32g	27
Muffins (toasting) average, 67g	28
Muffins, white Hyfibe, 67g	28
Rice Cakes, average	10
Taco shell/Tortilla, average, 18g	11

CAKES

	GMS CH
Cake, plain, average, 1 medium slice, 40g	20
Cake, plain, average, 1 large slice, 60g	30
Icing, average, 1 tbsp, 20g	12
Black Forest, 1 slice, 100g	40
Chocolate cake, 1 slice, 60g	28
Cupcake, iced, 40g	23
Donut, cinnamon/sugar, 70g	28
Donut, iced, 80g	39
Fruit cake, 50g, slice	27
Muffins, 1 medium, 60g	33
Iced fruit bun, 90g	42
Apple pie, 150g	40
Chocolate éclair, 60g	20

CEREALS

KELLOGGS

All-Bran, ⅓ cup	22
Bran Flakes, ¾ cup	24
Corn Flakes, Crunchy Nut Cornflakes, 30g	26
Coco Pops, Froot Loops, 30g	27
Just Right, ⅔ cup	24
Komplete Muesli, ¼ cup	23

	GMS CH
Mini Wheats, Whole Wheat (21)	25
Nutri-Grain, ¾ cup	22
Rice Bubbles, 1½ cups	26
Special K, ¾ cup	22
Sultana Bran, ⅔ cup	24
Sustain, ½ cup	24
SANITARIUM	
Up & Go, 250ml	25
Corn Flakes, 30g	24
Golden Toasted Muesli, ¼ cup	16
Good Start, each, 24g	19
Granola, ⅔ cup, 30g	20
Lite 'n' Tasty, 30g	23
Lite Bix, 2 bix, 30g	20
Puffed Wheat, 1½ cups, 30g	22
Soy Tasty, 30g	22
Weet-Bix, 2 bix, 30g	20
Weet-Bix Hi-Bran, each, 20g	11
UNCLE TOBYS	
Bran Plus, ½ cup, 30g	22
Flakes Plus, Lite Start, 1 cup, 30g	23

	GMS CH
Flakes Plus, Fibre Plus, 1/3 cup, 30g	23
Fruity Bites, 30g	25
Honey Grinners, 30g	25
Natural Swiss Muesli, 30g	20
Nut Feast, 30g	22
Oatflakes, 30g	24
Weeties (Original, Fruit 'N' Nut), 30g	21
Barley bran, 2 tbsp, 15g	9
Oat bran, 2 tbsp, 15g	8
Rice bran, 2 tbsp, 15g	7
Wheat bran, 2 tbsp, 20g	2
Wheat germ, 2 tbsp, 15g	5
Porridge, cooked, ¾ cup, 170g	19
Psyllium husks, 2 tbsp, 10g	1
Rolled oats, raw, ¼ cup, 30g	19
Muesli, average, 2 tbsp, 30g	17

CHEESE

Natural/Plain	0
Kraft Lite, Extra Lite singles, each	1

CHOCOLATE

CHOCOLATE, AVERAGE, ALL BRANDS, MILK/DARK/WHITE

Plain, 30g (5-6 pieces)	19
Plain, 100g block	62
Plain, 250g block	155
With nuts, 100g block	55
With fruit and nuts, 100g block	60
Cadbury Lite, 75g block	5.5
Carob bar, 50g	31

CHOCOLATE BARS

Aero Bar, 30g	17
Bounty, 50g	30
Cherry Ripe, 55g	24
Crunchie, 80g	60
Kit Kat, 4 wafers, 45g	27
M & M's, milk choc, 50g	34
M & M's, with peanuts, 50g	29
Maltesers, 45g pack	28
Mars Bar, 60g	42
Milky Way, 25g	18
Smarties, small pack, 25g	19
Violet Crumble, 50g	38

CONFECTIONERY

	GMS CH
Boiled sweets, barley sugar, average, each	5
Caramels, toffees, each	4
Chewing gum, pellets, each	1
Chewing gum, sticks, each	3
Sugar free chewing gum, Extra, Freedent, Jila	0
Sugar free chewing gum, Glean, Stimorol, Vapors	0
Jelly beans, babies, black cats, each	3
Licorice, 1 stick, 30g	17
Life Savers, 1 pack	24
Minties, each	4
Sugar free: Ricci Mint Drops	0
Jols Sugar Free Pastilles, 3	1
Kaiser Menthol/Wild Cherry	0

DESSERTS

Apple Crumble, 100g	37
Cheesecake, 1 large serve, 100g	30
Creamed Rice, ½ cup, 150g	25
Custard, baked, ½ cup, 145g	17
Fruche, 200g	25
Fruit salad, 1½ cup, 150g	20

	GMS CH
Jelly, regular, ½ cup, 120g	22
Jelly, low joule, ½ cup, 120g	0
Pancakes, three 10cm, 90g	27

EGGS

1 egg, plain	0
2 eggs, scrambled with milk	2
1 egg, omelette with tomato	3

FATS & OILS

Butter, margarine (all types)	0
Oils, all types	0

FRUIT, Dried

Apricots, 5 medium halves, 30g	13
Dates, 4 medium, 30g	20
Figs, 2 medium, 30g	16
Prunes, 4-5 medium, pitted, 30g	18
Raisins, sultanas, 30g	22

FRUIT, Fresh

Apple, 1 small with skin, 100g	12

	GMS CH
Apple, 1 medium with skin, 150g	18
Apricot, 1 small, 30g	2
Apricot, 1 medium, 40g	3
Apricot, 1 large, 60g	4
Avocado, ½ small (180g whole)	3.5
Avocado, ½ medium (240g whole)	5
Banana, 1 small, 100g	20
Banana, 1 medium, 150g	30
Banana, 1 large, 200g	40
Blackberries, ½ cup, 80g	10
Cherries, 15 large/25 small, 100g	12
Custard apple, ½ medium, 200g	32
Fruit salad, canned, ½ cup, 120g	13
Grapefruit, ½ medium, 100g	5
Grapes, average, all types, 1 small bunch, 22 medium, 120g	18
Guava, 1 medium, 120g	4
Kiwi fruit, 1 medium, 100g	10
Lemon, ½ medium, 75g	7
Loquat, 2 small, 40g	2
Lime, 1 medium, 70g	7

	GMS CH
Lychees, raw, 10 medium, 100g	17
Mandarin, 1 small, 80g	6
Mandarin, 1 medium, 120g	10
Mandarin, 1 large, 180g	14
Mango, ½ medium, 100g flesh	13
Mulberries, ½ cup, 100g	4
Nectarine, 1 medium, 90g	6
Olives, pitted, 6 medium, 50g	2
Orange, 1 small, 150g	12
Orange, 1 medium, 230g	17
Orange, 1 large, 300g	24
Passionfruit, 1 medium, 50g	3
Papaya, ⅓ medium, 100g	7
Pawpaw, ⅓ medium, 200g (peeled)	14
Peach, 1 medium, 115g	7
Peach, 1 large, 225g	14
Pear, 1 small, 115g	14
Pear, 1 medium, 150g	18
Pear, 1 large, 200g	24
Persimmon, 1 medium, 100g	16
Pineapple, 1 slice, 2.5cm thick, 86g	7

	GMS CH
Plum, 1 small, 50g	4
Plum, 1 medium, 100g	8
Plum, 1 large, 120g	9
Raspberries, ½ cup, 50g	11
Rhubarb, cooked, sweetened, ½ cup, 125g	37
Rockmelon, ½ small, 400g	9
Strawberries, 10 medium, 100g	3
Tamarillo (Tree Tomato), 75g	3
Tangelo/Tangerine, 1 medium, 160g	12
Tomato, 1 small, 100g	3
Tomato, 1 medium, 150g	4
Tomato, 1 large, 200g	5
Watermelon (no skin), 1 cup, 200g	10

ICECREAM

Icecream, average, all types, 1 scoop, 100ml/50g	11
Icecream cone, single	4

LENTILS, PEAS & BEANS

Lentils, raw, 100g	53
Lentils, cooked, 100g	17
Chick peas, raw, 100g	50

	GMS CH
Chick peas, cooked, 100g	22
Split peas, dried, raw, 100g	45
Split peas, cooked, 100g	22
Beans: Borlotti, brown, cooked, 100g	23
Broad beans, butter, cooked, 100g	2
Haricot beans, lima, cooked, 100g	13
Mung beans, cooked, 100g	18
Red kidney beans, cooked, 100g	10
Soybeans, cooked, ½ cup, 100g	9
3 or 4 bean mix, 100g	14
Baked beans, in tomato sauce, 100g	17
Baked beans, in tomato sauce, ½ cup, 150g	26

MILK & MILK DRINKS

Whole, low/non-fat, 1 tbsp, 20ml	1
Milk, whole, low/non-fat, 1 cup, 250ml	12
Powdered, whole/skim, 4 tbsp, 30g	10

POWDERED MILK DRINKS (Aktavite, Quik, Milo etc)

Average, 2 heaped teaspoon, 10g	7
Cocoa, 2 heaped teaspoon, 10g	2.3
Soy, Aussie Soy, all varieties, 250ml	19

MUESLI BARS, HEALTH SNACKS

Muesli bars/slices, average, all brands:

	GMS CH
Plain, 1 bar/slice, 95g	55
Carob/Yoghurt topped	65
K-Time (Kellogg's), Just Right	28
Uncle Tobys, muesli bars, average	21

NUTS (Shelled)

Almonds, 25-30 nuts, 30g	1
Brazil nuts, pecans, 30g	1
Cashews, 12-16 nuts, 30g	5
Coconut flesh, 30g	1
Coconut, dessicated, 1 tbsp, 8g	2
Coconut milk, 1 cup, 250ml	14
Peanuts, 30g	3
Pine nuts, macadamia, 30g	1
Pistachio nuts, dried, 30g	2
Walnuts, 30g	1

PASTA & NOODLES

Spaghetti, macaroni, fettuccine, cooked, 1 cup, 150g	37
Spaghetti, macaroni, fettuccine, brown, cooked, 1 cup, 150g	37

Spaghetti, canned in tomato sauce, ½ cup, 150g	17
Noodles, egg, cooked, 100g	25
Lasagna, 1 serve, 300g	35
Ravioli, 10 pieces, 70g	10

RICE & FLOURS

Barley, pearled, raw, 100g	61
Rice, white, cooked, 1 cup, 150g	42
Rice, brown, cooked, 1 cup, 150g	48
Flour, wheat, white, 100g	73
Flour, wholemeal, 100g	55
Wheat, whole, cracked, 100g	71

SNACKS

Burger Rings, 50g pack	31
Cheezels, 50g pack	29
Corn chips, average, 50g pack	31
Popcorn, popped, plain, 1 cup, 8g	4
Potato chips, average, 50g pack	25
Lite potato chips, average, 50g pack	28
Pretzels, 10 sticks, 8cm long, 6g	5
Twisties, average, 50g pack	30

SOFT DRINKS, CORDIALS

	GMS CH
Cola drinks, 375ml can	40
Lemonade, 7-Up, 375ml can	40
Bitter Lemon, Passiona, Jolt Cola, 375ml can	43
Fanta, Pinto, Sunkist, 375ml can	48
Dry ginger ale, 375ml can	28
Tonic water, 375ml can	34
Soda water, 375ml can	0
Diet low joule, average, 375ml can	1
Mineral water, plain, 375ml	0
Mineral water, flavoured/sweetened, average, 375ml can	38
Cordials (diluted 1:4) sweetened, 200ml	18
Diet Cordials eg Weight Watchers, 200ml	1.5

SPREADS

Jam/marmalade, 1 tbsp, 24g	8
Jam/marmalade, IXL Homestyle, 1 tbsp, 15g	8
Jam/marmalade, IXL Light conserve, 15g	4
Jam/marmalade, Weight Watchers, 1 tbsp, 15g	3
Honey, 1 tbsp, 24g	20
Golden/Maple syrup, 1 tbsp, 24g	18
Vegemite, Promite, Marmite,1 teaspoon	1

	GMS CH
Peanut butter, Kraft, 1 tbsp, 20g	4
Peanut butter, Sanitarium, 1 tbsp, 20g	2.5

SUGAR

Sugar, white/raw, 1 level teaspoon, 5g	4
Sugar, white/raw, 1 tbsp, 16g	16
Fructose/glucose, 10g	10
Sugar substitute, Equal, tab	0
Sugar substitute, Equal, sachet (equiv. 2 teaspoons sugar)	1
Splenda, 1 teaspoon	0.5
Sugarine, tablets, liquid	0
Stevia drops	0

TAKE-AWAY FOOD

Chicken, rotisseried/BBQ'd, ¼ chicken	0
BBQ chicken, with stuffing ¼ chicken	7
Chicken nuggets, 6 pack with sauce	24
Chicken roll, 300g	14
Chicko roll, 165g	44
Chips, 1 bucket, 150g	39
Dim sim, small, 50g	13
Fish and chips	95

	GMS CH
French fries, small, 80g	28
French fries, large, 110g	40
Hamburger, large, 250g	54
Hamburger, small, 180g	43
Hog dog	31
Pastie, 175g	26
Pie, meat, 175g	25
Pie, vegetarian, average, 200g	32
Sausage roll, large, 130g	35
Sausage roll, party size, 40g	26
Pizza, pan fried, average, 2 slices, medium	70
Pizza, thin base, average, 2 slices, medium	54
MCDONALDS	
Big Mac	43
Cheese Burger	35
Bacon and Egg McMuffin	28
Junior Burger	29
McOz Burger	48
McChicken	55
Quarter Pounder with Cheese	43
Apple Pie	

HUNGRY JACK'S	GMS CH
Whopper	52
Bacon Double Cheese/Deluxe	31
Aussie Burger	55
Grilled Chicken Burger	32
Whopper (Junior)	33
KFC	
Burgers, average	40
Chips, small, 120g	33
Fried chicken, portions: drumstick/wing, average	3
Fried chicken portions: breast/rib/thigh, average	6
Mashed potato and gravy, small	12
Nuggets, 6 pack with sauce	19
SUBWAY	
"6 Under 6" subs, average, with white bread	44
"6 Under 6" subs, average, with wheat bread	42

VEGETABLES

Artichoke, globe, 200g	3
Artichoke, Jerusalem, 4 small, 100g	3
Bean sprouts, 1 cup, 100g	2
Beans, French/Runner, ½ cup, 60g	3

	GMS CH
Beetroot, 1 medium, 120g	10
Broccoli tips, ½ cup, 60g	3
Brussel sprouts, 4-5, ½ cup, 70g	1
Cabbage, cooked, ½ cup, 40g	4
Capsicum, 1 medium, 140g	3
Carrot, 1 medium, 140g	7
Carrot, ½ cup, sliced/diced, 70g	4
Cauliflower, ½ cup, 100g	2
Celery, 1 piece, 15cm long, 30g	1
Chilli, 1 pod, 20g	1
Chives, chopped, 2 tbsp, 20g	1
Choko, ¼ medium, 60g	2
Corn, cooked, ½ cup, 90g	23
Corn, 1 ear, 125g	29
Cucumber, ½ cup slices, 50g	2
Eggplant (aubergine), 2 slices, 60g	2
Garlic, raw, 3 cloves, 9g	3
Lettuce, average, 2 leaves, 30g	1
Leeks, bulb and leaf, 30g	1
Marrow, 100g	3
Mixed vegetables, frozen, ½ cup	6

	GMS CH
Mushrooms, button, ½ cup, 60g	1
Mushrooms, umbrella, ½ cup, 60g	4
Onion, 1 medium, 120g	6
Parsnip, ½ large, 100g	10
Peas, fresh ¾ cup, 100g	8
Snow peas, 30g	1
Potato, peeled, 1 small, 100g	13
Potato, with skin, 100g	14
Pumpkin, Queensland blue, 100g	8
Pumpkin, butternut (no skin) 100g	7
Silverbeet, ½ cup, 100g	1
Spinach, ½ cup, 100g	1
Spring onion, 2 only, 20g	1
Squash, button	3
Swede, 100g	3
Sweetcorn, raw, ½ cup, 100g	15
Sweetcorn, canned kernels, drained, 100g	18
Sweetcorn, creamed style, 100g	17
Sweet potato, ¼ small, 100g	17
Tomato (see Fruit), 1 medium, 150g	4
Turnip, white, 100g	3

	GMS CH
Zucchini, 1 small, 100g	2

TOFU, TEMPEH, MISO

Miso, ½ cup, 140g	40
Tempeh, 1 piece, 85g	10
Tofu, firm, 100g	3
Tofu, soft/silken, 100g	2

SAUCES

Apple, 1 tbsp	5
BBQ., 1 tbsp	10
Chilli, 1 tbsp	10
Gravox, dry 25g	15
Hoisin, 1 tbsp	7
Horseradish, 1 tbsp	2.5
Mustard, 1 tbsp	1
Pasta sauces, 1/3 cup	11
Soy, 1 tbsp	0.5
Tomato, 1 tbsp	5.5
Vinegar, 1 tbsp	9
Worcestershire, 1 tbsp	4

*Some brands may vary—these are a guide only.

*Carbohydrate Counters are available in most newsagents and bookstores.

TESTIMONIALS

Testimonials from people who already have tried the *Power of Protein*.

Both in our mid 40s with a little 'middle aged spread' to shift we decided to give this diet a go. Well here we are a few weeks later, both down to our goal weights and feeling pretty damn good! Simon has lost 15 kilos and I have lost 8. We did this mostly without being able to cook 'normally' as we are in the process of renovating our kitchen. Thank God for the barbecue! Some of the side effects for me have been amazing. I have been asthmatic all my life and have found over the last few weeks less need to use the puffers. Also, an irritating eczema on my hands has complete gone. I'm wrapped! I have recommended your book to several friends who have all started on the diet themselves—even my parents in South Australia are into it. I am ordering another book today to send to my overweight niece in New Zealand. Many thanks for writing such a brilliantly simple and easy to follow book. I look forward to seeing another one on the shelves soon.
Julie—Gympie Qld

I have been overweight for most of my life and have dieted half heartedly for most of that time. When I never got results I always gave up. This diet has made it easy—the food recommended was the food I would normally eat anyway. I have lost a total of 24 kg and am totally indebted to you. I thought I was happy being overweight and had come to terms that I was never meant to be thin, but since losing weight I have a new found confidence and zest for life.
Jo

I recently saw a copy of your book and borrowed it from a friend. After following it for a week I am pleased to say I lost 3 kilos and of course purchased my own book. Many thanks.
Kaye—Adelaide SA

Your book has been fantastic. I have been following it now for a number of weeks and have lost 7 kilos painlessly! I have another 7 kilos to go before I reach my goal and I am quite confident I will survive Christmas.
Lottie—Brighton Vic

I am 5'7" and weigh 81.5 kg. I work fulltime and am a mother of a 16 month old girl. I am getting married next year and am hoping to get into a size 12 wedding dress. Since I started your eating plan—just 1 week ago—I have lost 3 kgs. What is so good is I'm not hungry anymore and I don't have sugar cravings! I have tried other plans and they were too hard to follow and not suitable to my family lifestyle, whereas this plan is flexible and I can enjoy the food with my family. I am sending a copy to my mother as she wants to look good as the mother of the bride.
Esther—Strathpine Qld

My name is Adrian and a friend of mine introduced me to your booklet 'The Power of Protein' about 5 weeks ago and I wanted to let you know I have had great results—so far I have lost 15 kilos. I am a married Italian man and all my life I have eaten lots of bread, rice and heaps of pasta. I have a very physical job as a roof carpenter—walking and carrying timber most of the day and I now have so much energy. I even went to the doctors to have a major physical checkup as I had lost the weight so quickly but the doctor was very impressed and said I am as fit as can be. So many of my friends are all so impressed and I tell them to go get 'The Power of Protein'. I would like to say thank you for turning my life around. Thank you.
Adrian—Perth WA

I decided to try the diet after my sister and brother-in-law raved about it and how much weight they had lost. After a short while I started the program and have never looked back since. I lost 3-4 kg in the first two weeks and since being on maintenance, I have not only kept the weight off but also lost a little more. I feel this is the best weight loss program I have been on and will recommend it to people I know.

Edith—Alexandra Hills

I have been following your low carb / high protein diet for 5 weeks and have lost exactly 8 kilos. I saw your book in the newsagents and decided I had to buy it. It was exactly what I needed—low carb tasty recipes. I now have so much energy and feel so much better since I went low carb.

Karen—Newcastle NSW

"The Power of Protein" is fantastic! I have been a yo-yo dieter since I was 20, now 50 years old. 30 years of trying all the major weight loss companies had left me pretty despondent (and fatter) at the lack of permanent results. This diet is wonderful! I am not tired, hungry or irritable and the weight loss is amazing. My husband and I have both lost weight—5 kilos in 4 weeks. The recipes are fantastic, the book is easy to understand and the results are brilliant! Thank you!

Cathryn—Tom Price WA

A friend of mine gave me a copy of your book two and a half months ago and asked me to give it a go. I was a bit sceptical at first as I had tried many diets in the past and I was never able to stick to the strict eating plans and subsequently put the weight back on. I have been following your plan now for 2 months and have gone from 107 kg to 94 kg in that time. I am surprised at how easy your plan is and the success I have achieved—so far with no exercise. I have a long way to go but thanks to you I now see a light at the end of the tunnel.

Melanie

INDEX